Feminine Consciousness in the Modern British Novel

Sydney Janet Kaplan

Feminine Consciousness in the Modern British Novel

University of Illinois Press
Urbana Chicago London

Publication of this work was supported in part by a grant from the Andrew W. Mellon Foundation

LIBRARY OF CONGRESS CATALOGING IN PUBLICATION DATA

Kaplan, Sydney Janet, 1939–
    Feminine consciousness in the modern British novel.

    Includes bibliographical references and index.
    1. English fiction—20th century—History and criticism.
    2. Women in literature. 3 Women's writings,
    English—History and criticism. I. Title.
PR888.W6K3   823'.03   75–2179
ISBN 0–252–00463–9

In memory of my mother
Frieda Kaufman Zendell

Acknowledgments

Brief portions of this book have appeared in a different form in articles in *College English* (May, 1971) and *Contemporary Literature* (Autumn, 1973).

I am grateful for the help I received from a number of people during the long process of writing this book. John Espey inspired me from the beginning and encouraged me to write about the feminine consciousness. Rosamond Lehmann sent me valuable suggestions about my chapter on her novels. The librarians in the Interlibrary Loan Department of the Research Library at UCLA helped me to track down many obscure novels. Ellen Levine assisted me with the index. Edward Kaplan, my husband, listened and understood and had patience.

Contents

Introduction: Feminine Consciousness and Female Characters

IN ENGLAND during the first quarter of the twentieth century two movements reached their climax and converged. One was literary: the experimentation with modes of consciousness in the novel; the other was social: the feminist struggle for equality and independence. Women were living in a period of transition; they were achieving some degree of economic and social freedom, but they were still expected to conform to traditional concepts of femininity. The cultural changes they had brought about were being conveyed through the medium of the popular realistic novel, but the effect of those changes on their psyches could not be expressed in this form since the larger share of the conflict lay beneath the surface within their divided consciousnesses. Thus it soon became apparent that the more fitting vehicle for interpreting the present reality of women's lives would be a novel of consciousness. It is not at all surprising, therefore, to find women writers among the important innovators of the modern novel.

Along with their male counterparts—James, Conrad, Proust, Joyce—a few women writers were also expressing dissatisfaction with the conventional novel. They found it necessary to break with tradition by shifting their focus from the outer world to the inner, from the confident omniscient narrator to the limited point of view, from plot to patterning, and from action to thinking and dreaming. But these women had also a more immediate concern than the purely aesthetic. The feminism of their contemporaries in the social and political arenas was to be reflected in their writing. They felt the need to consider consciousness not only as a means of organizing a novel but as a method for analyzing the minds of women and for attempting to define a specifically "feminine consciousness."

That urge to overcome the inadequacies of external realism had a very special meaning, I believe, for these early twentieth-century women writers. Dissatisfied with the characterizations of women in current fiction, they wanted to go beyond stereotypes, and to attempt to create whole selves in their fiction that went past abstractions that separate feeling and thinking. With them, one finds an urgency to express the importance, the value of individual perceptions, what Thomas Hardy long ago defined in relation to his Tess as "her precious life." Hardy remarked that "upon her sensations the whole world depended to Tess; through her existence all her fellow-creatures existed, to her. The universe itself only came into being for Tess on the particular day in the particular year in which she was born."[1]

How to write about those "sensations," however, was the very problem the early moderns tried to solve. Hardy recognized the need for considering it but could not approach a re-creation of those sensations from the inside—at least not from within Tess herself, who for all her complexity still remains close to a "concept" of woman. But the writer who aims for a total sense of lived experience, who recognizes that it is through characters' consciousnesses that it may be depicted, is confronted with numerous difficulties. To explore *any* character's "stream of consciousness" involves certain assumptions. If an inner life is to be revealed, how should it be structured? What principles govern the course of that "stream"? And the question most essential to our purpose here may be: if the character whose consciousness we are to explore is female, what must the author do to make her consciousness "feminine"? Are there really *inherent* differences

1. Thomas Hardy, *Tess of the D'Urbervilles* (1891; reprint, New York: New American Library), pp. 170–71.

between the consciousnesses of men and women? Finally, is it even possible to know, if biology, psychology, and anthropology all present us with such various and generally conflicting answers?[2]

Fortunately, we do not have to resolve that ultimate question in order to consider the literary problem. For we do start with one fact, and that is that novelists have most definitely attempted to depict the consciousnesses of men and women and to show that each has a different quality. In order to do this they have, inescapably, brought to these depictions certain assumptions about the psychic differences between men and women that have much to do with the shapes these depictions of consciousness ultimately assume. Consequently, when I use the term "feminine consciousness" here, I hope the reader understands that I am using it in a rather special and limited way. I use it not simply as some general attitude of women toward their own femininity, and not as something synonymous with a particular sensibility among female writers. I am concerned with it as a literary device: a method of characterization of females in fiction. In fact, I will go even further and say that I am not using "feminine consciousness" even so broadly as to take in the full range of any given woman's consciousness in a novel, but only those aspects of it which are involved with her definition of self as a specifically feminine being. That is why I use the adjective "feminine" to modify "consciousness" rather than "female."[3] The latter simply refers to the biological condition of being a woman; the former connotes charac-

2. See, for example, Naomi Weisstein, "Psychology Constructs the Female, or the Fantasy Life of the Male Psychologist," in Elaine Showalter, ed., *Women's Liberation and Literature* (New York: Harcourt, Brace, 1971), pp. 271–86. But even questions about behavioral differences between the sexes are problematic, let alone psychic ones. Robert J. Stoller in *Sex and Gender: On the Development of Masculinity and Femininity* (New York: Science House, 1968) opposes theories of innate differences between men and women in terms of behavior. He says that ". . . insofar as the development of gender identity is concerned in almost all humans, by far the most powerful effect comes from postnatal psychodynamic factors" (p. x). For a full account of available research, see Eleanor E. Maccoby, ed., *The Development of Sex Differences* (Stanford: Stanford University Press, 1966).

3. My distinction here between "female" and "feminine" is similar to Robert Stoller's use of the terms in distinguishing sex and gender: "*Gender* is a term that has psychological or cultural rather than biological connotations. If the proper terms for sex are 'male' and 'female,' the corresponding terms for gender are 'masculine' and 'feminine'; these latter may be quite independent of (biological) sex" (p. 9).

teristics which, though usually ascribed to women, derive not only from their physical makeup but from a combination of physical traits and socially based attitudes about what constitutes femininity. After all, there is a difference between a "female body" and a "feminine figure." The first is fact, the second opinion. When considering "feminine consciousness," one must never forget all the ways in which the beliefs of the author about what constitutes femininity of mind have gone into the structuring of consciousness of any given female character.

In this study I am concerned with the ways in which the consciousnesses of women are organized in the novels of women writers. In particular, how do the female characters in the novels evolve their own specifically feminine consciousnesses? My focus is thus not on the authors' own consciousnesses but on how they develop uniquely feminine ones for their women characters. I have chosen five British novelists whose works span the past seven decades in order to analyze how notions of "feminine consciousness" emerge, develop, and change over a period of many years. Since I have considered only novelists who have experimented with techniques which probe the interior lives of women, who consider in at least a limited fashion some aspects of what has been so loosely—and often incorrectly—termed the "stream of consciousness,"[4] I have neglected several well-known modern British women novelists. But this was necessary in order to relate these fictional definitions of feminine consciousness to the larger aesthetic problem of discovering methods with which to deal with consciousness itself. For one basic issue is the relationship between the views of life revealed in the novels and the particular forms in which consciousness is contained within them. Through an understanding of these relationships it becomes possible to in-

---

4. I use the term "stream of consciousness" rather loosely throughout this study, following more or less the definitions of Melvin Friedman and Robert Humphrey, who distinguish between the subject matter and the technique of stream of consciousness. For instance, Humphrey states, ". . . there is no stream-of-consciousness technique. Instead, there are several quite different techniques which are used to present stream of consciousness" (*Stream of Consciousness in the Modern Novel* (Berkeley and Los Angeles: University of California Press, 1965), p. 4). See also Melvin Friedman, *Stream of Consciousness: A Study in Literary Method* (New Haven: Yale University Press, 1955).

clude within the definitions of feminine consciousness some considerations about the creative process and the special problems of the woman artist, as well as the connections between "feminine" patterns of thinking and specific methods of artistic creation.

I begin with Dorothy Richardson's *Pilgrimage* for more reasons than simple chronology, even though its first volume, *Pointed Roofs* (written in 1913 but not published until September, 1915), is the earliest work of any of the five authors entirely centered in the consciousness of a female character. It was Dorothy Richardson who once identified her method as "the feminine equivalent of the current masculine realism."[5] And it is in *Pilgrimage* that one can most clearly discern the presence of traditional attitudes about the female psyche at the same time as one observes how those attitudes provide the basis for a new form of literature and a new method of character development. Dorothy Richardson sets a foundation of traditional attitudes, and these underlie the work of the other women in this study as well. Their characters also share in a conflict which is an inescapable part of their attempts to defend the feminine consciousness by defining it, clarifying it, and even perhaps deifying it. That conflict results from their need to retain the traditional division of consciousness—masculine reason and feminine intuition—and yet assert the superiority of the feminine component at the same time that they use "masculine" methods of discourse in order to explain it.

Although her first novels were written at the turn of the century, May Sinclair follows Dorothy Richardson here, because she was more an interpreter of Dorothy Richardson's method than an innovator in her own right; her own attempt at a stream-of-consciousness novel followed her reading of the first few volumes of *Pilgrimage*. Her novels are, unfortunately, nearly unknown at the present time, but she is important for this study because she organized, simplified, and communicated in a more popular form many of the theoretical concepts related to the fictional exploration of consciousness.

Since Virginia Woolf's contributions to the novel of conscious-

5. Dorothy M. Richardson, "Foreword" to *Pilgrimage*, I (New York: Alfred A. Knopf, 1967), 9.

ness are so immense, and the bulk of criticism devoted to them so vast, I have considered her writing within some rather strict limitations. I focus primarily upon only two of her female characters, Clarissa Dalloway and Lily Briscoe, and look at how they reveal definitions of themselves as women. These self-definitions, however, are distinguished by their incorporation of the notion of the "androgynous" mind, and by the blurring of some of the rigid categorizing of "feminine" and "masculine" capabilities. Virginia Woolf's concept of the androgynous is especially important in its connections with the process of artistic creation, and is treated here in this light.

I have included Rosamond Lehmann in this study for two reasons. First, she is the least theoretical writer of the group. The discoveries of the earlier women have been absorbed, accepted, and modified in her novels by the demands of the more conventional fictional patterns. Second, her novels deal with a later generation of women, and are useful in revealing the persistence of older beliefs about femininity and feminine consciousness which are greatly at odds with the lives of the women who hold them. Rosamond Lehmann's novels take this study into the forties and fifties and illustrate how the tension arising from the conflict between concepts and life styles continually increases.

The fifth novelist is Doris Lessing, and she brings this study up to the present. In fact, she leaves us an opening into the future in which the direction is not at all certain. Her characters represent a specifically contemporary definition of feminine consciousness, one which incorporates the tremendous social and political changes that have taken place during the last twenty years. Her concern with the fragmentation and disintegration of the feminine consciousness is of most importance here.

As a whole, this study is an attempt both to analyze specific definitions and to mark how they are affected by the passage of time and the influence of external events. I approach the subject initially by looking at the major female characters in these novels in terms of how they reveal their own definitions of feminine consciousness. But self-awareness only achieves a recognition of what is known to the conscious mind; these authors also attempt to define feminine consciousness in terms of what the characters do not know about themselves. It is necessary to analyze submerged feelings that are only revealed implicitly through imagery, emphasis, and shifts in tone. The very processes of thinking, the patterns of consciousness, are as important as the contents of the mind in this respect.

In general, my method is to analyze the separate components of the feminine consciousness as they are revealed through the structuring of the consciousness of individual women in the novels. One of the most important areas is that of sexuality. I consider how these women deal with themselves as physical beings and sexual objects, and try to link their attitudes toward physicality with their view of their relationship to nature. The second area involves these women's consciousness of their social role, and this includes the effect of that role upon their relationships with other people—men, women, and children. Finally, I consider the thinking process itself. How do these women order perceptions, and how do they conceptualize reality? What distinctions do they make between the way they see the workings of their own minds and the way in which they believe the minds of men operate? It is in this connection that the relationship between a "feminine" way of thinking and a "feminine" method of creativity is made apparent in these novels.

One

Dorothy M. Richardson

DOROTHY RICHARDSON's long series of novels, *Pilgrimage*,[1] might seem quiet and serene to a modern reader, but it was conceived in revolt against the established traditions of fiction. Dorothy Richardson (1873–1957) wrote from the beginning of her career to the end as a radical—not politically, by any means, but stylistically. Her writing marks a revolution in perspective, a shift from a "masculine" to a "feminine" method of exposition. The thirteen volumes of *Pilgrimage* are all organized around the consciousness of their main character, Miriam Henderson. All events are filtered through Miriam's brain by the use of a third-person narrator who looks into Miriam's mind and describes how it perceives life from moment to moment. Thus the perspective of the novel is limited; its point of view is contained within the powers of this young woman to see and analyze her own life. It is a novel of consciousness in both method and content. For through the method of consciousness itself, its main theme—the development of "feminine consciousness"—is revealed and defined.

1. Dorothy M. Richardson, *Pilgrimage* (New York: Alfred A. Knopf, 1967), with an introduction by Walter Allen. Vol. I: *Pointed Roofs* (1915), *Backwater* (1916), *Honeycomb* (1917); vol. II: *The Tunnel* (1919), *Interim* (1919); vol. III: *Deadlock* (1921), *Revolving Lights* (1923), *The Trap* (1925); vol. IV: *Oberland* (1927), *Dawn's Left Hand* (1931), *Clear Horizon* (1935), *Dimple Hill* (1938), *March Moonlight* (previously unpublished).

Like Henry James and Joseph Conrad, Dorothy Richardson used the device of limited perspective in order to explore the outer world through the perceptions of a particular character. Through these perceptions she hoped to come closer to reality than had the authors of the prevalent naturalistic and realistic novels written from an "objective," "scientific" method of observation. She was not opposed to their desire for realism, not at all. But she wanted to discover an even deeper realism, a realism which would incorporate a recognition of the limitations placed on knowledge of the external world. She was to join those who searched after reality by directing their attention to that obscure and endless life within the human mind. Doubting the accuracy of the senses, or their ability to perceive anything in its totality, they recognized the essential connection between the objects of the external world and the perceivers of those objects.

It has long been one of the commonplaces of literary criticism to say that Dorothy Richardson was the first English writer to use the "stream of consciousness,"[2] but she was to reject the term, once calling it "this more than lamentably ill-chosen metaphor,"[3] and again as a term "isolated by its perfect imbecility."[4] Shirley Rose has recently suggested a more workable definition of the form and content of *Pilgrimage*, calling it "a psychological novel depicting reality through the feminine consciousness."[5] She goes on to clarify Dorothy Richardson's position:

> In describing the phenomena of existence, including the passage of time, the construction and use of language, the verbal expression of ideas and feelings, the associational processes of thought —we are justified in using words like flux, flow, stream, as appropriate metaphorical equivalents. However, in speaking of the consciousness as Dorothy Richardson conceives of it, we require metaphors that indicate expansion without movement or change.

2. May Sinclair, "The Novels of Dorothy Richardson," *Little Review*, 4 (Apr., 1918), 3–11.
3. Dorothy M. Richardson, "Novels," *Life and Letters*, 56 (Mar., 1948), 189.
4. Stanley Kunitz, ed., "Dorothy Richardson," *Authors Today and Yesterday* (New York: H. W. Wilson, 1933), p. 562.
5. Shirley Rose, "The Unmoving Center: Consciousness in Dorothy Richardson's *Pilgrimage*," *Contemporary Literature*, 10 (Summer, 1969), 368.

We therefore must regard consciousness in spatial terms without the usual correlative of time.[6]

Shirley Rose's discussion is especially useful in relation to Dorothy Richardson's definition of "feminine consciousness," for Miriam's "pilgrimage" takes her from flux to stability. Yet the metaphor of the stream may still have some relevance in that the very bulk of the novel is largely taken up with those very "associational processes" which require the passage of time, and not with those moments of timelessness which may be more important but are less frequent occurrences. Moreover, Miriam's awareness of herself as a female being is also involved with socially derived conceptions that she becomes aware of through the interactions of mind and external phenomena. It is that interaction between mind and phenomena which Dorothy Richardson communicates through a method she once identified as the "feminine equivalent of the current masculine realism."[7] She wanted to write a realistic novel, but she defined "reality" in terms of a woman's perspective. She believed that "masculine" realism, with its emphasis on external appearances, logic, hierarchical categorizing, neglects the center of experience—the perceiving and reflecting mind.

But when Dorothy Richardson created a consciousness for Miriam, she did not merely demonstrate a feminine mode of thinking. Her radicalism is acted out through a definite assertion of the *superiority* of the feminine consciousness. Miriam begins her definition out of defiance at the evidence of masculine prerogatives that she sees everywhere around her. After all, her late Victorian adolescence coincides with a prevalent antifeminine mood. She has only to look in the encyclopedia to find the statement "woman is undeveloped man" (II, 220). All the authorities seem to assume that "civilization" is man's province.[8] It is no wonder that Miriam responds to men's belief in their own superiority with both hostility and despair:

6. *Ibid.*, p. 369.
7. Richardson, "Foreword," *Pilgrimage*, I, 9.
8. For examples of these attitudes, see selections in R. E. L. Masters and Eduard Lea, *The Anti-Sex: The Belief in the Natural Inferiority of Women: Studies in Male Frustration and Sexual Conflict* (New York: Julian Press, 1964).

If, by one thought, all men in the world could be stopped, shaken, and slapped. There *must*, somewhere, be some power that could avenge it all...but if these men were right, there was not. Nothing but Nature and her decrees. . . . [II, 220]

There was nothing to turn to. Books were poisoned. Art. All the achievements of men were poisoned at the root. The beauty of nature was tricky femininity. The animal world was cruelty. . . . Religion was the only hope. But even there there was no hope for women. No future life could heal the degradation of having been a woman. [II, 222]

Miriam's attempt to go beyond the prevalent belief in women's inferiority is complicated, however, by her own "masculine" attributes. She remarks about herself, "I am something between a man and a woman, looking both ways" (II, 187). Much of her hostility must be directed against that other side of herself. This makes it a double kind of hostility or opposition: against that other half of humanity who represent all the forces which suppress women, and also against that logical, classifying, intellectual part of herself which is so often at odds with her deeper, "intuitive" femininity.

Miriam's defensiveness is based partly on her own sense of inferiority and jealousy. Although she comes to experience a sense of freedom through the poverty of her own independent life, she yet observes how restricted life becomes for most women who live with their families. She resents men's lack of appreciation for women's values, for their inner qualities which she believes are superior to men's. Her anger sometimes surfaces through what may appear to be mere quibbling—an attempt to quarrel without showing overt hostility. For example, here is a seemingly random thought which quickly passes through her mind when she becomes frightened by the sound of fireworks: "Why do people always like a noise? Men. All the things men have invented, trains and cannons and things make a frightful noise" (I, 327).

But usually her attack is on a more serious level. She wants to get at men's smugness and certainty in their own values. To do this she must first deflate their achievements:

"Art," "literature," systems of thought, religions, all the fine products of masculine leisure that are so lightly called "immortal." Who makes them immortal? A few men in each generation who are in the same attitude of spirit as the creators, and loudly claim them as humanity's highest spiritual achievement, condoning, in those who produce them, any failure, any sacrifice of the lives about them to the production of these crumbling monuments. Who has decreed that "works of art" are humanity's highest achievement? [IV, 93]

Miriam's basic distinction is between the ways men and women use their thinking minds.[9] The "masculine" reliance on logic, categorization, rationality, is opposed to "feminine" intuition. All of Miriam's deepest hostility is apparent when she recognizes the blindness of men locked into their own conceptualizations:

Miriam's stricken eyes sought their foreheads for relief. Smooth brows and neatly brushed hair above; but the smooth motionless brows were ramparts of hate; pure murderous hate. That's men, she said, with a sudden flash of certainty, that's men as they are, when they are opposed, when they are real. All the rest is pretense. Her thoughts flashed forward to a final clear issue of opposition, with a husband. Just a cold blank hating forehead and neatly brushed hair above it. If a man doesn't understand or doesn't agree he's just a blank bony conceitedly thinking, absolutely condemning forehead, a face below, going on eating—and going off somewhere. Men are all hard angry bones; always thinking something, only one thing at a time and unless that is agreed to, they murder. My husband shan't kill me....I'll shatter his conceited brow—*make* him see...two sides to every question...a million sides ...no questions, only sides...always changing. Men argue, think they prove things; their foreheads recover—cool and calm. Damn them all—all men. [I, 437–38]

Miriam speaks always in favor of relativity even though she often expresses her own views dogmatically, not really accepting

9. Several critics have questioned the validity of Miriam's division of mental functioning into masculine and feminine components. See, for example, Robert Humphrey, *Stream of Consciousness in the Modern Novel* (Berkeley and Los Angeles: University of California Press, 1965), p. 11, and E. M. Maisel, "Dorothy M. Richardson's Pilgrimage," *Canadian Forum*, 19 (June, 1939), 91. The most favorable view is John Cowper Powys, *Dorothy M. Richardson* (London: Joiner and Steele, 1931), p. 17.

the "sides" of the question. What she usually objects to is some man's refusal to see *her* side or, even worse, to refuse to look at it because she is a woman. She cannot bear it when a man is not interested in her ideas; she is especially irritated when he communicates his lack of interest through belittling and condescension. Her employer, Mr. Hancock, is guilty of all of these failures:

> . . . he would not have patience to hear her try to explain; and by that he robbed her of the power of trying to explain. He was not interested in what she thought. Not interested. His own thoughts were statements, things that had been agreed upon and disputed and that people bandied about, competing with each other to put them cleverly. They were not *things*. It was only by pretending to be interested in these statements and taking sides about them that she could have conversation with him. He liked women who thought in these statements. They always succeeded with men. They had a reputation for wit. [II, 107–8]

Miriam believes these "statements" are never deeply original, perhaps because they are mechanical, built up out of previously accepted ideas, merely put together in a new way.

Miriam's own method does not conform to this pattern. A good way of seeing this might be to look closely at the following passage, which clearly illustrates what Miriam means by differing masculine and feminine intellects. Here she picks up a book written by a man, hurriedly glances at its first few paragraphs, and then proceeds to criticize its logic:

> Why did men write books? Modern men? The book was open. Her eyes scanned unwillingly. Fabric. How did he find his words? No one had ever said *fabric* about anything. It made the page alive...a woven carpet, on one side a beautiful glowing pattern, on the other dull stringy harshness. . . . "There is a dangerous looseness in the fabric of our minds." She imagined the words spoken, "looseness" was ugly, making the mouth ugly in speech. There is a looseness in the fabric of our minds. That is what he would have said in conversation, looking nowhere and waiting to floor an objection. "There is a *dangerous*," he had written. That introduces another idea. You were not supposed to notice that there were two statements, but to read smoothly on, accepting. It was

deliberate. Put in deliberately to frighten you into reading more. Dangerous. . . . People who read books do not think about *adjectives*. They like them. Conversation is *adjectives*! ...All the worry of conversation is because people use adjectives and rush on..... But you can't describe...but "dangerous" is not a descriptive adjective...."There is a twisted looseness," that describes...that is Saxon...*Abendmahl*...dangerous, French...the Prince of Wales uses the elegant Norman idiom...."Dangerous" is an idea, the language of ideas. It expresses nothing but an opinion about life...a threat daring you to disagree. Dangerous to what?...Man is a badly made machine...an oculist could improve upon the human eye...and the mind wrong in some way too...logic is a cheap arithmetic. *Imagination*. What *is* imagination? Is it his imagination that has found out that mind is loose? Is not imagination mind? It is his imaginative mind. A special kind of mind. But if mind discovers that mind is unreliable, its conclusion is also unreliable. That's logic. . . . All mind is unreliable. Man is mind, therefore man is unreliable....Then it is useless to try and know anything. . . . But he did not invent "dangerous." That is cheek. By this sin fell the angels. Perhaps he is a fallen angel. [II, 407–8]

The passage is a long one, but I have quoted it nearly in full because I believe that several crucial features of Miriam's consciousness are apparent in it. For instance, at the beginning there is her sudden jumping on the word "fabric" as a counterpoise to "dangerous." The one is concrete, evoking images, the other abstract, evoking ideas. She attacks the illogic of the phrase through this linguistic analysis, always coming back to the specific, the concrete meanings of the words which lead most certainly to absurdity when she visualizes them. Her own "logic" depends, then, upon analysis of meaning rather than syllogisms. But even she resorts to syllogisms as her mind runs on: "All mind is unreliable. Man is mind, therefore man is unreliable." This obviously ironic thrust at the absurdity of deductive reasoning becomes part of Miriam's emotional response, a response which is always a major part of her criticism. She makes no attempt at "objectivity." Her initial focus on the words leads her outward in an associative pattern to consideration of adjectives themselves, social opinions (Prince of

Wales—snobbery), and then imagination itself, the mind, and finally, as the focus widens, to man's pride and false superiority.

But all this is leading somewhere. Miriam's associations point up an underlying statement about the very central difference between the thinking of the sexes—that is, men's obsession with things and women's with people. Men's rigid categorizing, their putting of ideas into order in hierarchies of importance, places a material value upon them. These account for what Miriam calls "the absence of personality" (III, 280) among men. She believes it is not due to their experiences in the world, not to "environment," but to something essential in men: "It is original. Belonging to maleness; to Adam with his spade; lonely in a universe of *things*" (III, 280).

Miriam believes that man creates civilization out of a need to escape from his own loneliness. He is lonely because he is unable to participate completely in the present moment, as does woman; and he is lonely because he cannot absorb the diversity of experience possible in any given moment of time:

> It is man, puzzled, astray, always playing with breakable toys, lonely and terrified in his universe of chaotic forces, who is pitiful. The chaos that torments him is his own rootless self. . . . Men weave golden things; thought, science, art, religion, upon a black background. They never *are*. They only make or do; unconscious of the quality of life as it passes. . . . Men have no present; except sensuously. That would explain their *ambition*...and their doubting speculations about the future. [III, 280–81]

Woman avoids this loneliness and the sense of constantly impending chaos which makes man construct his world of things for protection. That is because her understanding of "life," her immersion in the processes of nature and human intercourse, allows her to be deeper and more responsive to the forces of the universe. She sees the world of women as boundless, not limited by the ordering imposed by masculine conventions. Yet women seem so fragile, so unpredictable, so flighty, that men usually infer that they need conventions: "Women's controls appear to be

feebler because they have so much more to control. I don't mean
physically. Mentally. By seeing everything simultaneously. Unless
they are the kind of woman who has been warped into seeing only
one thing at a time. Scientifically. They are freaks. Women see
in terms of life. Men in terms of things, because their lives are
passed amongst scraps" (III, 393).

The difference between women's inner view of experience and
the outward view of men is traditionally associated with the worlds
each inhabits. The most common pattern has men dealing with
the outside world through work, and women with home, family,
and religion. Years after Dorothy Richardson had already utilized
and refined this conventional attitude toward the consciousnesses
of men and women, she was able to bring the added support of
psychological opinion to it. In an essay written in 1929 she cites
Jung's "persona" and "anima" as the psychological basis for the
division. In this article she speaks of the uniqueness of the feminine psyche with its " 'shapeless' shapeliness," which is "its power
to do what the shapely mentalities of men appear incapable of
doing for themselves, to act as a focus for divergent points of
view."[10] It is this capacity for "being all over the place and in all
camps at once"[11] which allows woman to be able to live completely in the present. In this way Dorothy Richardson was able
to make the major distinguishing feature of the feminine consciousness explicit: the ability to perceive both the diversity of
experience and its immediacy.[12]

II   The basic component inherent to Dorothy Richardson's
       concept of the feminine consciousness as it is developed
throughout *Pilgrimage* is Miriam's strong ambivalence toward
her role as a woman. It is this ambivalence which charges with

10. Dorothy M. Richardson, "Leadership in Marriage," *Adelphi*, 2nd ser., 2
(June–Aug., 1929), 347.
11. *Ibid.*
12. Particular aspects of Dorothy Richardson's use of a feminine point of view,
especially its quality of passivity, are discussed by various critics, especially Frank
Swinnerton, *The Georgian Scene* (New York: Farrar & Rinehart, 1934), p. 387,
and Lawrence Hyde, "The Work of Dorothy Richardson," *Adelphi*, 2 (Nov.,
1924), 512, and "Proust, Joyce, and Miss Richardson," *Spectator*, 130 (June 30,
1923), 1084–85.

tension the attempted demarcation of feminine and masculine aspects of consciousness. It causes a separation between the verbalized, intellectual, and abstract statements Miriam makes about the feminine consciousness and her actual emotional reactions to situations in her life. This ambivalence is so important as a force behind any complete understanding of the concept that it is not going too far to say that it, more than anything else, is the primary ingredient in her development of a "feminine consciousness."

The source for this ambivalence might be Miriam's earliest determining influences. She is the third of four daughters. Her parents had longed for a boy and had treated her as if she fulfilled that expectation: "Within me...the *third* child, the longed-for son, the two natures, equally matched, mingle and fight? It is their struggle that keeps me adrift, so variously interested and strongly attracted, now here, now there? Which will win?" (III, 250).

She prefers to identify herself with her father because her mother is a weak and dependent person. In addition, her mother's conventional expectations for her daughters go against Miriam's drive for independence. Besides, her father understands those same qualities in women that irritate and alienate her: "women's smiles—smirks—self-satisfied smiles as if everybody were agreed about everything. She loathed women. They always smiled. . . . Pater knew how hateful all the world of women were and despised them" (I, 21–22). She recognizes this same quality in herself. "I am a misanthrope," Miriam at seventeen remarks, "so's pater. He despises women and can't get on with men. We are different —it's us, him and me. He's failed us because he's different and if he weren't we should be like other people" (I, 31).

Her father's failure, brought about by his scorn for the advice of others, his sense of superiority, and perhaps his snobbishness, although it makes him a romantic in Miriam's mind, in reality provides yet another impediment toward her realization of a conventional feminine role. His failure is essentially a financial one, and because of it—ironically fortunate, as it turns out—Miriam must become independent. She had always seemed independent when compared with her sisters and friends; that independence derived from her masculine expectations. But with her father's bankruptcy, Miriam is forced to be financially independent as well. In this way she is pushed into experiences which necessitate "masculine" determination and ingenuity if she is to make her way in the world. Although she is very young, she sees herself as "the strong-minded one" (I, 30) and knows "it must be the end of taking money from him. She was grown up" (I, 30).

Miriam strikes out on her own but never loses the defiant, uneasy stance of the first, lonely rebel. All around her are other women—buying dresses, taking long walks with their children, hurrying home to prepare tea—comfortable, attractive women, women belonging to men. Objects they may be, dependent, limited, but their lives have an ease that is missing from her own. In order to live happily with the frugality of her own life, Miriam must turn it into a superior value. She must guard her freedom very carefully; she must treasure her independence, for she is always aware of that "other" way of life beside her. And she also knows that from the vantage point of the "typical" woman, her own life must seem very strange indeed. "Always, in relation to household women, she felt herself a man. Felt that they included her, with a half-contemptuous indulgence, in the world of men" (III, 412).

The words "half-contemptuous" and "indulgence" are projections which reflect Miriam's ambivalence toward ordinary women. These words also reveal that her attitude toward them is based not only on her very different style of living but also on her fears that she might be inferior to those women in terms of grace and beauty.[13] She grew up feeling that way with respect to her three sisters. She always thought she was not as pretty as the others.

13. One of the more amusing commentaries on Miriam's sexual inadequacies is the following: "Nature was in a satirical mood when she equipped Miriam for her conflict. . . . Plain in appearance, angular in manner, innocent of subtlety, suppleness, or graciousness of body or soul, with a fine sensitiveness fed by an abnormal self-appreciation, which she succeeds in covering only at the cost of inducing in it a hot house growth. . . . Tortured by romantic sentimentalism unrelieved by a glimmer of imagination or humour; over-sexed but lacking the magnetism without which her sex was as bread without yeast" (Joseph Collins, "Dorothy Richardson and Her Censor," in *The Doctor Looks at Literature* (New York: Doran, 1923), pp. 105–6).

Her ambivalence as a woman grows out of this sense of physical uneasiness as much as her identification with her father. Perhaps her insecurity about her own body may account for the rather peculiar absence of body consciousness in some parts of the early novels.[14] Some of the reticence might very well be attributed to the remnants of Victorian standards of decorum. In this light, a description of Miriam's first menstrual period in *Pointed Roofs* (1915) might be considered relatively advanced:

> She remembered with triumph a group of days of pain two years ago. She had forgotten....Bewilderment and pain...her mother's constant presence...everything, the light everywhere, the leaves standing out along the tops of hedgerows as she drove with her mother, telling her of pain and she alone in the midst of it... for always...pride, long moments of deep pride....Eve and Sarah congratulating her, Eve stupid and laughing...the new bearing of the servants...Lilly Belton's horrible talks fading away to nothing.
> [I, 137]

What may strike a modern reader is the lack of physical detail here, the kind of detail Doris Lessing includes in *The Golden Notebook*, for instance. But I don't think anyone would call it pathological, considering when the novel was written. Miriam's memory of her first period, recounted in flashes separated by ellipses which make it shadowy and abrupt, allow a definite sense of her pride in her new womanhood to shine through. It becomes a statement of power, of overcoming the inhibitions implicit in "Lilly Belton's horrible talks."

But the lack of physical detail in many of the scenes of sexual encounter is what seems most disturbing. For example, when much later, in *Deadlock* (1921), Miriam is kissed by Michael Shatov, the kiss is never described. In fact, the reader does not

14. Walter Allen has commented upon the peculiar absence of bodily references in *Pilgrimage*: "There are whole areas of a woman's experience—every woman's experience—Miriam is never allowed to be conscious of. The bodily functions do not exist for her; in this respect, she is at one with the most conventional Victorian heroine of fiction. And the stream-of-consciousness technique makes us more aware of this. It is unfair, but it is next to impossible now not to think that Dorothy Richardson cheated" (*Tradition and Dream* (London: Phoenix House, 1964), p. 15).

know until later that Miriam has even been kissed at all. Instead, Miriam's thoughts show that she is focused on her own mental state and emotional condition rather than on her physical sensations:

> The long moment was ending; into its void she saw the seemings of her grown life pass and disappear. His solid motionless form, near and equal in the twilight, grew faint, towered above her, immense and invisible in a swift gathering swirling darkness bringing him nearer than sight or touch. . . . She ceased to care what thoughts might be occupying him, and exulted in the marvel. Here, already, rewarding her insistence, was payment in royal coin. She was at last, in person, on a known highway, as others, knowing truth alive. . . . The encircling darkness grew still, spread wide about her; the moving flames drew together to a single glowing core. The sense of his presence returned in might. The rosy-hearted core of flame was within him, within the invisible substance of his breast. Tenderly transforming his intangible expansion to the familiar image of the man who knew her thoughts she moved to find him and marvel with him. [III, 192]

Several features can be distinguished in this passage, the most noticeable being the lack of physical description. The reader is nearly teased into guessing what is going on. And the ambiguity which results allows the imagination to go much further than the kiss itself. What opens up here is the whole area of sexuality for Miriam. The kiss is merely a limited symbol for it. Thus its description is not necessary and would, in fact, detract from the expansion of the symbol to the larger areas which it then may encompass. The passage is noteworthy for its sense of movement, the swirling, ever-moving pace of a journey into the unknown. The images of fire and glowing, magic and transformation, all contribute to the boundlessness of the experience, giving it an almost mystic quality. The style can be defended as sufficient for its purpose, as the inclusion of physical detail would weaken it and make it seem trite, ordinary. Nevertheless, this passage still reveals elements of Miriam's basic insecurity as a woman. In a way it is similar to her reaction to beginning menstruation: surprise and wonder at something most women expect and believe to be typical. Her first physical contact with a man makes her see herself as finally "on a known highway," recognizing "the celebrated nature of her experience." At last she may accept herself as a woman like other women.

Whenever other people accept Miriam as a normal woman, she seems surprised. Their acceptance draws her out, pleases her, but her pleasure conflicts with her desire to be unique and independent. At the same time that she finds herself carried away by Michael's attraction to her, she senses his intrusion into her autonomy. Gradually she begins to resent his compliments. Once she even tells him that she will never marry, and he responds with, " 'You think you will never marry...with *this*'—his ungloved hands moved gently over the outlines of her shoulders. 'Ah—it is most— musical; you do not know' " (III, 303). Miriam quickly understands that his flattery merely destroys her individuality and makes her into a physical object. It pulls her directly away from her desires to be like other women, because for her to accept her sexuality as they do, to become a vessel for the sensual pleasures of men, is repugnant:

> She thrilled to the impersonal acclamation; yet another of his many defiant tributes to her forgotten material self; always lapsing from her mind, never coming to her aid when she was lost in envious admiration of women she could not like. Yet they contained an impossible idea; the idea of a man being consciously attracted and won by universal physiological facts, rather than by individuals themselves. [III, 303]

Miriam continues to vacillate between rejecting her physicality and desiring its acceptance. When a man admires her, she responds with uneasy pleasure which turns her attention once again to her own body, of which she is usually unaware: "Her happy blush revealed to her the shape of her body—as if for her own contemplation, as if her attention were being called to an unknown possession that yet was neither hers nor quite herself—glowing

with a radiance that was different from the radiance of the sur-
rounding sunlight . . ." (IV, 149–50). Her awareness here is still
not related to a consciousness of any *specific* physical sensations
or observations. The description she makes of herself involves
"the shape of her body" but not a concrete perception of that
shape itself.

It is not until Miriam's affair with Hypo Wilson—her only
affair which culminates finally in sexual intercourse—that she
thinks about her particular physical attributes in detail. At that
point, her ability to direct attention openly to her body indicates
that she is becoming able to accept herself physically as well as
mentally. It assures her that she is as beautiful as other women;
she has attracted a famous man who is celebrated as much for his
sexual adventures as for his writing. Thus, in the following passage, the reader might not perceive the same level of ambivalence
about her sexuality that Miriam reveals elsewhere. This is not
only because she is overwhelmed by Hypo's interest in her, but it
is also a response to her newly developed self-image that has been
encouraged by her friendship with a young woman, Amabel. She
is able, then, to respond without hostility to Hypo's compliment
—" 'You *are* a pretty creature, Miriam. I wish you could see yourself' "—with an internal image of herself that is fortified by Amabel's approval:

> With the eyes of Amabel, and with her own eyes opened by
> Amabel, she saw the long honey-coloured ropes of hair framing
> the face that Amabel found beautiful in its "Flemish Madonna"
> type, falling across her shoulders and along her body where the last
> foot of their length, red-gold, gleamed marvellously against the
> rose-tinted velvety gleaming of her flesh. Saw the lines and curves
> of her limbs, their balance and harmony. Impersonally beautiful
> and inspiring. To him each detail was "pretty," and the whole
> an object of desire.
>
> With an impersonal sacredness they appeared before her, less
> imaginable as objects of desire than when swathed, as in public
> they had been all her life.
>
> This mutual nakedness was appeasing rather than stimulating.
> And austere, as if it were a step in some arduous discipline. [IV,
> 231]

Miriam is still uneasy here about what will come from her sexuality. She is as close to accepting her own body as she will ever be, but she cannot go any further. While she is able to think about her "limbs" and "flesh" and "hair," she is able to do so by distancing herself from them, by making them "impersonally beautiful and inspiring." They are things which belong to her yet can never be considered part of her. She is unable to continue a physical description of her sexual feelings up to their actual conclusion. Although she finally has sexual intercourse with Hypo Wilson, the reader is not presented the fact directly. It is only later, when she refers briefly to the new change in her life after returning to London, that the reader is made to understand that Miriam is no longer a virgin. It is almost as if her "stream of consciousness" disappeared underground for a short period of time. What she is able to consider, however, is the effect that experience had upon her. And here again, the effect enhances her self-image. Again she stresses how she feels like other women, how she is now a part of the processes of natural humanity. Through such phrases as "disadvantage had fallen from her and burden, leaving a calm delightful sense of power," and "she was full of inward song and wishing for congratulations" (IV, 267), the reader becomes aware of what has happened and observes that Miriam once again rests in confidence that she has passed the test of womanhood.

Another facet of Miriam's ambivalence involves behavior that is often more maternal than sexual.[15] She often finds herself in a maternal role with men because she believes that basically she is stronger than most men and certainly superior to them.[16] When Miriam comforts Michael after he has disappointed her by ad-

15. See Gloria Glikin, "Dorothy Richardson's Pilgrimage: A Critical Study" (dissertation, New York University, 1961), p. 173. She points out that Miriam only relates to Shatov in "the maternal role."

16. This sense of superiority is related to a "concept of masculine blindness and male ineptitude—a concept which originated in the image of her father" (Horace Gregory, *Dorothy Richardson: An Adventure in Self-Discovery* (New York: Holt, Rinehart & Winston, 1967), pp. 26–27). Gregory relates many of the details in *Pilgrimage* to events in Dorothy Richardson's own life. Other biographical details may be found in Gloria Glikin's article, "The Personal 'Pilgrimage,'" *PMLA*, 78 (1963), 586–600. The recent and only full-length biography is John Rosenberg's *Dorothy Richardson* (New York: Alfred A. Knopf, 1973).

mitting his earlier sexual relationships, she loses her anger and finds herself consoling him:

> "Poor boy," she murmured, gathering him as he sank to his knees, with swift enveloping hands against her breast. The unknown woman sat alone, with eyes wide open toward the empty air above his hidden face. This was man; leaning upon her with his burden of loneliness, at home and comforted. This was the truth behind the image of woman supported by man. The strong companion was a child seeking shelter; the woman's share an awful loneliness. It was not fair. [III, 212]

Later, when she attempts her first sexual liaison with Hypo Wilson, their sexual encounter fails because Miriam's maternal feelings overtake her sexual ones. When she sees Hypo without his clothing, she suddenly becomes aware of his vulnerability:

> The impulse seemed reckless. But when she had leaned forward and clasped him, the warm contact drove away the idea that she might be both humiliating and annoying him and brought a flood of solicitude and suggested a strange action. And as gently she rocked him to and fro the words that came to her lips were so unsuitable that even while she murmured "My little babe, just born," she blushed for them, and steeled herself for his comment.
>
> Letting him go, she found his arms about her in their turn and herself, surprised and not able with sufficient swiftness to contract her expanded being that still seemed to encompass him, rocked unsatisfactorily to and fro while his voice, low and shy and the inappropriate unwelcome charm in it of the ineffectual gestures of a child learning a game, echoed the unsuitable words. [IV, 232]

The tenderness and sympathy which Miriam displays initially here, even though these qualities may interfere with her sexuality, are qualities which one must assume she considers to be part of the "feminine consciousness." [17] But as always, her response is di-

17. However, several critics have commented on a lack of tenderness and typical feminine virtue in Miriam. Mary Ellmann says that ". . . Dorothy Richardson is the least womanly, in any snug sense, of all women novelists. She looks into cradles and kitchens the way people look at the moon: Interesting, someone should go there" ("Dorothy Richardson's Pilgrimage," *New Republic*, 157 (Oct. 28, 1967), 23). But Mary Ellmann's appreciation for Miriam's honesty is worlds

vided: at first spontaneous, reckless, rocking the naked man, and then embarrassed, blushing at her sentimentality and already putting herself into a "masculine" frame of reference as she waits for his criticism.

Her whole relationship with Hypo Wilson is filled with contradictions. He is an unusual man, yet she rails against him more than she does against any other man in the novel. He is certainly willing to accept women in competing intellectual and economic roles. He is willing to accept a single standard of sexuality (a liberal one for both sexes). He does not have the same belief in a protective, patriarchal relationship with women that is so common among men of his day. But what Miriam cannot bear about him is his refusal to accept what she defines as the feminine way of thinking—intuition, mystical perception, multi-leveled consciousness—as real, or even preferable to masculine logic. He wants reason; his whole career is founded upon it. He believes that it is irrationality that has made the world so dreadful. Thus he pursues scientific goals, sees in organization the best future for humanity. Miriam finds herself revolting against his socialistic theories because she thinks they are too rational and orderly. She prefers to think of herself as a "Tory-anarchist." It is finally, almost painfully ironic that Hypo fails her because he comes closer than any other man to agreeing to the equality of the sexes.

But Miriam believes that his notion of equality assumes a masculine mode of thinking as its basis. Men and women are equal as long as women think like men! Somehow it is easier for her with other men whose attitudes are much more obvious. Michael Shatov might speak of female equality in intellect, but he assumes subordination within a sexual relationship. Miriam knew she could never marry Michael because she believed he would demand that she be a passive, accepting wife. Her suppositions are accurate, for later Amabel's role as Michael's wife takes on that very submissiveness that Miriam feared for herself.

---

away from the older, more traditional view, such as that of Pelham Edgar: "We must admit that Miriam's femininity lacks the quality of tenderness and the capacity for subordination that have hitherto been the distinguishing qualities of her sex" (*The Art of the Novel from 1700 to the Present Time* (New York: Macmillan, 1933), p. 328).

Yet in spite of Miriam's attempt to defend the superiority of the feminine consciousness, and her hostility against the privileges and presumptions belonging to the male sex, she is often attracted—against her ideals—to men who represent the conventional position, even to men who are *totally* committed to the concept of women's inferior role. First is her crush on her employer, Mr. Hancock, which never develops beyond her wishes and fantasies. And then much later she is attracted to the Quaker farmer, Richard Roscorla. That attraction is the most remarkable of all because of the vast differences in education and class. Miriam knows all the time that Richard would never be able to accept either her independent views or her "past." The closest she comes to allowing herself to take part in a conventional relationship, however, is with Dr. Densley, an intelligent yet nonintellectual physician. He appeals to her because of his traditional masculine attributes—strength and protectiveness:

> His wide, varied experience of humanity seemed all about them, as they wandered at truce arm-in-arm through the darkened evening streets. And she found herself, as always, leaning upon his ordered knowledge and yet repudiating it, so entirely did it imply an incomplete conception of life. Every symbol he used called up the image of life as process, never in any direction as completeness. . . . In life itself, the bare fact of life, there seemed for him to be no splendour. For men there was ambition, hard work, and kindly deeds by the way. And for women motherhood. Sacred. The way to it pure comedy; but once attained, life for the mother in a mansion of the spirit unknown to men, closed against them and for ever inaccessible. The attainment of full womanhood was farewell, a lonely treading of a temple, surrounded by outcasts. . . .
>
> The strange thing was that seeming to value her for what he called the intellectual heights that had kept her uncorrupted by petty social life, he yet wanted her to come down from them and join the crowd. [III, 476–77]

Densley views marriage as a means of dealing with the essentially tragic nature of life. At the same time it holds clear satisfactions for the woman who is worshipped for her role, a secretive one whose mystery is not to be penetrated by men. To Miriam, Densley's awe over the traditional role of women makes it less abhorrent in some ways than the companionate false equality she would experience with Hypo. At least men like Densley have a mystical appreciation for the sexual nature of women, something that may be accepted without logical proof. Paradoxically, this "something" is at odds with the very intellectual powers necessary for "equality" in the other sense of that term. Therefore, it is ironic that Miriam is less hostile toward a man who would really subject her to an inferior role, even if by so doing he might worship the sublime nature of that role.

Miriam is aware of some other advantages of the traditional relationship: appreciation for her physical beauty, protection, economic support, and, oddly enough, room for her own individuality in realms that are exclusively of a "woman's world." If the roles are clearly demarcated, there might very well be a fair amount of freedom within those roles. At the same time, however, Miriam recognizes the dangers behind her temptation: "There would be solace for all the wounds of thought in his unconsciousness. But no companionship. For a long while nothing at all of profound experience and then, perhaps, her whole being arranged round a new centre and reality once more accessible, but in a loneliness beside which the loneliness of the single life was nothing" (III, 489). Her internal freedom would then be at the price of isolation. If one accepts that the woman's world cannot be penetrated by man, that it is a mystical, intuitive realm which excludes him, then a woman must be alone in it.

What Miriam really desires is a man who could accept the feminine consciousness—accept its difference—and at the same time understand it. What she would most like is for men to become like women in their minds, to become feminine in their thinking. Then there would be no more isolation. Women are already able to think masculinely; they learn that method through all their contacts with education. But men have not made a similar excursion into the world of the female mind. The way to reconcile the differences between men and women, according to Miriam, would be for men to understand women's special attributes:

"The thing most needed is for men to *recognize* their illusion, to drop, while there is yet time, their newest illusion of life as only process. Leave off trying to fit into their mechanical scheme a being who lives all the time in a world they have never entered. They seem incapable of unthinking the suggestions coming to them from centuries of masculine attempts to represent women only in relation to the world as known to men." [IV, 92]

III   Miriam's basic insecurity in her feminine role is closely re-lated to her confused relationships with other women, which grow out of that early masculine self-identity as the "son" of her family. Since she is so aware that she is different from other women, she usually finds her relationships with them awkward and tense. Her feelings vacillate between a violent woman-hating (and here she blames women for their weakness, their acceptance of an inferior role, their insincerity, and their instability) and a romantic idolization of woman, complete with emotionality, self-abnegation, and desire. She must compete with women and yet too often finds herself shortchanged because she seems to lack "femininity." Thus she must either raise herself above the women she fears by despising them and casting doubt upon their values, or accept her latent masculinity and avoid competition with women by denying her inadequacies and taking on the male role. As a man she would not have to compete with beautiful women—only to idolize them. As a consequence, Miriam expresses several obsessions with various women throughout *Pilgrimage*. In fact, one might even say that her obsessions with women contain more desire, and more explicit direct expression of emotions, than her heavily intellectualized discussions of her relationships with men. It seems that here lie her most direct feelings. This is not to imply that Miriam should be viewed as a lesbian. Rather, one may see in her ambivalence over her role as a woman many elements of latent homosexual feelings. These complicate and cloud her division of consciousness into masculine and feminine components even further.

One side of Miriam's feelings for women grows out of an intense hostility, often revealing itself when she realizes that she is in a losing competition. At such times it breaks out in a repressed fury, such as during one day when she was teaching at the Misses Perne's school. She was confronting two students who were talking during study time:

> With beating heart Miriam got up and went and stood before them. "You two are talking," she said with her eyes on the thickness of Polly's shoulders as she sat in profile to the room. Eunice, opposite her, against the wall, flashed up at her her beautiful fugitive grin as from the darkness of a wood. History, thought Miriam. What has Eunice to do with history, laws, Henry II, the English Constitution? "You don't talk," she said coldly, feeling as she watched her that Eunice's pretty clothes were stripped away and she were stabbing at her soft rounded body. [I, 288]

It is in such a scene that Miriam's submerged feelings of anger are allowed to come to the forefront of her mind. Usually her consciousness excludes them. But here the feelings are too strong, and they well up through the images which are not verbalized internally. The stabbing image occurs at the same time in her consciousness as the verbalized statements about history and Henry II. Flashing images of this sort do not occur very often, and when they do, they often conflict with the explicit statements Miriam frames in her conscious mind. Dorothy Richardson joins these two levels of Miriam's mind together quite effectively, in order to reveal the painful, unexpressed feelings that cause Miriam such inner turmoil, turmoil she tries to keep in order through her processes of rationalization.

At the root of Miriam's problem is her need to compete with other women. But this competition works also in a different way than merely trying to outdo another woman. Since she has a dual nature—masculine as well as feminine—she often understands the feelings of a man when he is involved with a woman. Thus her competition is rather sympathetic; she can understand and even feel the same attraction for another woman that a man might feel. During her relationship with Hypo Wilson, Miriam had to face the prospect of competition with his wife, Alma, who also happened to be her old school friend. Torn two ways, Miriam rationalizes that Hypo lost sexual interest in Alma a long time ago. But she likes Alma, is attracted to her. She retains a deep appreciation for those very qualities in Alma which must have attracted Hypo to her in the first place. By identifying herself with Hypo's masculine point of view, she forgets about competing and merely adores the same woman Hypo once loved. And she even mixes her adoration with a kind of masculine condescension as well, complimenting Alma's "deep magnetic radiance" at the same time as she subtly underrates it: "Receiving this radiance fully for the first time, Miriam felt she could kneel, with the world's manhood, in homage to the spirit of the womanly woman, yet shared, as the radiance passed, their cramped uneasiness, the fear that makes them flee, once they are committed to the companionship of these women, from the threat of being surrounded and engulfed in insufficiency" (IV, 162).

Miriam's relationship with the nurse, Eleanor Dear, reveals another part of her complex psychological situation. In this case Miriam is involved with a woman who is totally dependent, always in trouble, has a bad reputation, and is charming, flighty, and courageous. Her intellectual level is far below Miriam's, and her experiences and background place her in an entirely different class. But with her Miriam can indulge all kinds of feelings of power and superiority, of kindly intervention and incisive analysis. She is not "in love" with Eleanor in the way she later becomes with Amabel. She does not dote on their similarities; it is clearly a relationship with dominant-subordinate partners. But Miriam can test her own values according to Eleanor's, and can try out her growing sense of control and influence over others on Eleanor as well. Yet this control and influence actually reveal how totally Miriam has become obsessed with Eleanor. When Eleanor is around, there is no one else. She possesses Miriam through the power of her weakness. Miriam becomes isolated from others in a world of Eleanor Dear. And she senses the power Eleanor has over her—the power of Eleanor's open acceptance of whatever happens to her—and Miriam is fascinated with this. Once, when Eleanor returns after a long absence, Miriam remarks, "It was part of her mystery that she should have come back just that very afternoon. Then she was in the right. If you are in the right everything works for you. The original thing in her nature that made her so beautiful, such a perpetually beautiful spectacle, was *right*" (III, 282).

Miriam only maintains a sense of distance from Eleanor—this amoral woman whose beautiful and tragic nature makes her so appealing—through the help of her own "masculine" analytical mind. She keeps trying to analyze, to define, to describe, to categorize Eleanor's qualities:

> It is tempting to tell the story. A perfect recognizable story of a scheming unscrupulous woman; making one feel virtuous and superior; but only if one simply outlined the facts, leaving out all the inside things. Knowing a story like that from the inside, knowing Eleanor, changed all "scandalous" stories. They were scandalous only when told? . . . To call Eleanor an adventuress does not describe her. You can only describe her by the original contents of her mind. Her own images; what she sees and thinks. She was an adventuress by the force of her ideals. Like Louise going on the street without telling her young man so that he would not have to pay for her trousseau. [III, 285]

This kind of internal story-telling, gossiping almost, is common in *Pilgrimage*. But its purpose goes deeper. This passage performs several functions, not the least of which is how it reflects Miriam's need to describe—and to distance herself through describing. In order to do any of it she must use some forms of masculine discourse, in particular, logically sequenced words themselves. But she uses them in order to show that they are limited and unsatisfactory. She works through a criticism of the words themselves. Knowing that a word like "adventuress" is merely a label for a predetermined set of character, and that character cannot be "summed up" so simply, she recognizes that there are many layers to any observation. One must see both the inside and outside, the images as well as the externals. To get part of the complexity across involves doing more than labeling, putting into categories. Her process is first to cast doubt upon the very hope of ever knowing everything. Because if one realizes that a label cannot define Eleanor Dear, then it also cannot describe situations. Thus "scandalous" becomes suspect. Typically, Miriam goes on, philosophically questioning speech itself. She returns to Eleanor and tries to use words to convey something too complex to describe in statement. She finally ends up with an analogy that gives the spirit of Eleanor's "adventuring" but does not define it. (Miriam uses imagery or analogy frequently, especially when she attempts to express her sense of inadequacy of language.)

Miriam's obsession with Amabel exemplifies how her need to compete with a beautiful woman may be handled by repression. She pretends, or rather does not notice, that the cause for competition exists. She can eliminate here that painful experience of being judged in relation to the "other," by making that "other" become one with herself. What evolves with Amabel is a rather narcissistic, inward-turning mutual admiration[18]—a sense of total oneness, an enjoyment of complementing characteristics that, combined, seem to make for perfection. And this oneness allows for an escape from the isolation of the self, and from having to accept her own revelations of insufficiency. But the relationship is beneficial because it allows Miriam to release her feelings and to experience some kind of communion with another human being. It allows her to recognize the common humanity in another and to be able to experience it at the same time. Furthermore, it permits her to get out of the trap of constant rationalizing and isolated thinking, by experiencing that thinking through another's reactions. All of these help Miriam to grow and to become less defensive about her femininity. What is more, the very recognition of Miriam's femininity by Amabel—Amabel who notices her attributes and appreciates them, who makes her aware of her feminine feelings—eventually will allow Miriam to experience what sexual adventures she finally does have. It was impossible for her to identify with Eleanor Dear's sexual experiences, but not so impossible to do so with Amabel, who is an independent, dynamic, educated woman. Now she can see the possibilities within sexuality, experience the recognition of her own deep female instincts in another woman, then be able to transfer them to herself, create the dynamic energy which eventually leads Miriam to experiment and not to fear.

18. Miriam's obsession with Amabel was preceded by one for Ulrica during her stay in Germany. See *Pilgrimage*, I, 74.

The sense of total oneness that Miriam achieves with Amabel grows out of the special kind of communication they establish with each other right from the beginning of their relationship. Miriam is so attracted to Amabel that she is aware that "the room had seemed filled with golden light giving an ethereal quality to all its contents" (IV, 188) during her first conversation with the younger girl. The "ethereal quality" derives in part from the unspoken intensity of their immediate communication. It proves instructive to follow Miriam's pattern of thinking during this first encounter. When Amabel gets close to her, she does so by using a subtle kind of flattery:

> "Yes, you are English, that is the strange thing," she remarked in a polite, judicial tone, "and so *different*," she added, head sideways, with an adoring smile and a low voice thrilling with emotion. Her hands came forward, one before the other, out-stretched, very gently approaching, and while Miriam read in the girl's eyes the reflection of her own motionless yielding, the hands moved apart and it was the lovely face that touched her first, suddenly and softly dropped upon her knees that now were gently clasped on either side by the small hands. [IV, 190]

Miriam's consciousness here is aware of the sound of the words Amabel utters and the way they are uttered—including, most important, the physical manifestations that accompany these words. There is a movement in her consciousness from a direct apprehension of the words themselves, to an interpretation of the emotions accompanying the words, to a direct apprehension of their physical manifestations, to an interpretation of their meaning. Miriam's awareness of herself occurs simultaneously with her perception of Amabel. The next paragraph intensifies Miriam's self-awareness:

> Alone with the strange burden, confronting empty space, Miriam supposed she ought to stroke the hair, but was withheld, held, unbreathing, in a quietude of well-being that was careless of her own demand for some outward response. She felt complete as she was, brooding apart in an intensity of being that flowed refreshingly through all her limbs and went from her in a radiance that seemed to exist for herself alone and could not be apparent to the hidden girl. [IV, 190]

The intensity of this passage, with its expectant mood, static and yet trembling, reveals Miriam's release from a constricted sense of herself, giving her energy because she has let go of self-imposed boundaries to her self-concept. It is this release—this opening up of boundless possibilities in the simultaneous merging and paradoxically delineating quality of their union—which is its dynamic and motivating force. Miriam's awareness of the power in her attraction for Amabel also includes the insight that she will now no longer be the same:

> Her current life had grown remote and unreal. . . . Seeing herself reflected in the perceptions of this girl, she was unable to deny, in the raw material of her disposition, an unconscious quality of the kind that was being so rapturously ascribed to her. But it was not herself, her whole current self. It belonged to her family and her type, and for this inalienable substratum of her being she could claim no credit. Yet in being apparently all that was visible, and attractive, to this socially experienced and dis-illusioned and clear-eyed young woman, it seemed to threaten her. She could feel, almost watch it coming forth in response to the demand . . . feel how it kept her sitting perfectly still and yet vibrant and alight from head to feet, patiently representing, authentic. And a patient sadness filled her. For if indeed, as her own ears and the confident rejoicing that greeted every word she spoke seemed to prove, this emerging quality were the very root of her being, then she was committed for life to the role allotted to her by the kneeling girl. [IV, 191–92]

Amabel has flattered her, appealed to her deepest egocentricity, and embarrassed her. No one has done this for Miriam before; she needs the confidence that grows out of a kind of idolization of herself. But Miriam here moves away from the rhapsodic qual-ity of the first paragraph because she is aware of her own awareness of the limitations on what Amabel sees. Yet she wants to trust it, wants to believe in its accuracy. And it gives her faith to accept a power in herself which is reflected in this girl whom she begins to idolize. Amabel has the social charms which Miriam always felt she lacked: femininity, beauty, sexual appeal. And if Amabel recognizes these same qualities in Miriam, not only recognizes them, but deepens them with the addition of wisdom and intuition, then perhaps Miriam will be able to look at herself in a new way. But she is frightened. It is easier to be the old Miriam, easier not to set herself too high, to take no chances.

Their relationship explodes with Miriam's realization of the intense feelings involved in it. This explosion does not destroy the relationship, but cements it in a new combination: a deep, passionate friendship which approaches the fury of a love affair.

Amabel writes the words " 'I love you' " on a mirror, and this declaration of love allows Miriam's obsession to overwhelm her and draw her into a nearly complete absorption with the younger woman. Amabel becomes so important that she affects all of Miriam's perceptions, heightening them so that they often produce creative and unusual insights. But these insights come in spurts; Miriam's analytical abilities focus now on narrower fields, such as Amabel's handwriting, for example:

> Alive. These written words were alive in a way no others she had met had been alive. Instead of calling her attention to the way the pen was held . . . instead of bringing as did the majority of letters, especially those written by men, a picture of the writer seated and thoughtfully using a medium of communication, recognizing its limitations and remaining docile within them so that the letter itself seemed quite as much to express the impossibility as the possibility of exchange by means of the written word, it called her directly to the girl herself, making her, and not the letter, the medium of expression. Each word, each letter, was Amabel, was one of the many poses of her body, upright as a plant is upright, elegant as a decorative plant, supporting its embellishing curves just as the clean uprights of the letter supported the curves that belonged to them. [IV, 215]
>
> . . . Real. Reality vibrating behind this effort to drive feeling through words. [IV, 217]

Miriam takes one of Amabel's characteristics, her handwriting, and uses it almost symbolically as the emblem for her character. As we shall see later, according to Miriam's definition of the feminine consciousness, this kind of symbolizing is a very "feminine" method of character analysis, considering, as it does, the self as an unchanging, unanalyzable quality which is beyond logical apprehension. "Each word, each letter, was Amabel" makes personality almost mystical, something revealed by all the manifestations of the physical—as well as mental—activity of the self. "Reality vibrating" is what Miriam always wants to approach and experience, and it is no wonder that discovering it in the other woman enriches her friendship. Yet it is also such a powerful experience that it serves to isolate her, now in a new kind of isolation—an isolation in duality. The "mysterious interplay" (IV, 217) takes her beyond all her past associations. It will make everything else pale and delusive: "But now to-morrow morning and all the visible circumstances of her life had retreated to inaccessible distance, leaving her isolated with this girl. Suddenly, punctually isolated, as once she had been with Eleanor, and again this time, just as everything about her had become a continuous blossoming" (IV, 217).

Ironically, it is through Miriam's efforts to relate her relationship with Amabel to Hypo Wilson that it begins to take its real shape in her life. The more she is drawn to Hypo and the more she compares him with Amabel, the clearer becomes the one-sided nature of her isolating experience with Amabel. At first she uses Amabel as a weapon against Hypo and his intrusion into her life; she sets Amabel up against him as a rival. This permits her to push him away at the same time as she tantalizes him: " 'I'm preoccupied,' she said. 'Perpetually, just now, with one person. . . . It's treasure, beyond your power of diagnosis. Beyond any one's power' " (IV, 240). How fitting that Miriam needs to undermine Hypo's masculine "power of diagnosis"! Her preoccupation allows her to add fuel to the already roaring fire built out of her hostility toward men. Now she may boldly assert her independence from them. She believes that a man is not capable of seeing the "real" Amabel, or the "real" Miriam either. She fantasizes, however, about what Hypo's reaction to Amabel might be: "She looked at Amabel through his eyes. And saw almost everything in her escape them. Her poses and mannerisms, that were second nature, he would amusedly accept as so many biological contrivances. And if he thought her 'pretty'—sacrilege, even in thought, to apply to

Amabel this belittling expression that at this moment I see as part
of his deliberate refusal to take any kind of womanhood seriously
. . ." (IV, 240). There is an interesting switch from the third to
the first person in this passage. Miriam assumes that she sees
through Hypo's eyes as she imagines his typical responses. Yet in
the last sentence the sudden use of "I" directs attention to Miriam
and not to Hypo's supposed thoughts. This awkward shift allows
Miriam's anger at his blindness to break through. In that anger,
a direct quote from her deeper consciousness comes bursting forth.

Her anger is not only at Hypo and his limited perspective but
at herself and her failure to communicate the reality of her relationship with Amabel. It hurts her to realize that Hypo will
probably come away with only "a shadowy idea of Amabel's quality and a definite picture of two young women engrossed in one of
those mysterious sudden intimacies that precede the serious affairs
of life and end, 'at the touch of reality,' as swiftly as they had
begun" (IV, 247). And yet she wants him to know, even though
it may belittle him, that "nothing . . . could compare with what
Amabel had brought. Nothing could be better. No sharing, not
even the shared being of a man and woman, which she sometimes
envied and sometimes deplored, could be deeper or more wonderful than this being together, alternating between intense awareness of the beloved person and delight in every aspect, every word
and movement, and a solitude distinguishable from the deepest,
coolest, most renewing moments of lonely solitude only in the en-
hancement it reaped by being shared" (IV, 242).

This isolating experience with Amabel is as intense an experience as she will ever know. But she remains defensive about it,
revealing that defensiveness through her attempt to put the very
things she fears about the relationship into Hypo's own words,
making them seem oversimplified, blind, and unacceptable. Of
course she knows that the mystical essence that makes her friendship special cannot last and that "Amabel will move on." To
blunt the pain of that realization, she thinks about the positive
changes in herself brought about through knowing Amabel: "She
stands permanently in my view of life, embodying the changes
she has made, the doors she has opened, the vitality she has added

to my imagination of every kind of person on earth" (IV, 251).

What makes her knowledge of the impending break-up of their relationship—at least its most intense aspects—so painful is that she believes she will never have this kind of intensity with a man. Yet she cannot go on forever in a self-reflexive fixation. She needs a man, and she needs the balance of his differences.

Although Miriam's friendship with Amabel gradually becomes more conventional, less emotional, the obsessive feelings for women that are a part of her ambivalent nature are not lost, merely supplanted by other feelings. Long after her affair with Hypo has ended, even after her involvement with the farmer, Richard Roscorla, has ended, Miriam again finds herself in a situation that calls forth those intense feelings for another woman. Miriam's friendship with Jean (in the last volume of *Pilgrimage, March Moonlight*) follows a similar pattern to the one with Amabel. But now Miriam is older, well into her thirties, and she does not easily retain the quality of delayed adolescence that was obvious during her "romance" with Amabel. There was a sensual quality in her attraction to Amabel; she was absolutely "in love" in the self-absorbed manner of an adolescent. The obsession seemed to incorporate all the repressed sexual energy that she had not yet released. In contrast, the relationship with Jean only *seems* romantic. It contains some of the same elements: the unspoken understandings, the meaningful silences, the building up of philosophical justifications for feelings. Here again is the obsessiveness, the spontaneous awareness of each other, and the growing isolation. But with Jean these relate to a mystical rather than a psychological communion. This difference is due partly to Miriam's age and experience and partly to her recent discovery of religion, which includes her new awareness of a pantheistic God and the sense of humanity built up out of her experience with Quaker fellowship and community at Dimple Hill. Her new state of mystical awareness is a state of absolute feminine consciousness. She believes she shares this with Jean, expressing it in phrases like "The moment we found ourselves together, time stood still" (IV, 567) and "To return to Jean is to find oneself at an unchanging centre" (IV, 566).

However, Miriam is misled in this relationship. Caught up in the mysterious atmosphere of the involvement, Miriam discovers that Jean is not so totally immersed. She has been using the friendship as a way of making herself available to men. Miriam reacts to her discovery with all the hurt feelings of a rejected lover (reverting to her earlier concept of "friendship"). She even attempts to rationalize the break with Jean according to religious principles, to lessen the sense of hurt and to avoid looking too deeply at the possible betrayal:

> Good that she is gone. How right are the Catholics in separating within their orders those who grow too happy in each other. To give oneself, fully, to God-in-others, one must belong to no one. Careful though she was, and in the end taught me to be, to avoid, in public, any revelation of partiality, we yet aroused jealousies. As those last weeks slid away, the glow we created in each other could not be concealed.
>
> Jean. Jean. Jean. My clue to the nature of reality. To know that you exist, is enough. [IV, 612]

IV   Miriam's conflict between masculine and feminine roles, her desire for independence and feminine superiority, compete in various ways with her feelings for traditional values and behavior. As a result, she turns more and more to religious insights instead of rational observations as she matures. She begins to oppose the over-rationality of intellectuals, contrasting it with the intuitive awareness of people like the Quaker Roscorlas. She ties this growing sense of religious commitment to her view of the feminine consciousness. It is as if she accepts, at last, that part of herself which stems from her traditional background. But as much as she accepts it, she can never accept herself as totally a woman in the traditional sense.

It is clear, then, that as Miriam continues to confront the paradoxes of her position as a woman (that complex made up of attraction and repulsion, freedom and dependence, logic and intuition, ambivalences of several sorts), she senses the increasing need to preserve her sense of self. She guards it at every turn from infringements by others who might try to control her. As a result

—or perhaps as the cause—she has trouble becoming close to others. She is attracted to the isolation offered to her within the boundaries of the traditional marriage, and it tempts her before she finally rejects it. She rejects it because, ultimately, she wants communion, oneness with others. Yet she shies away from it, fears it. She is afraid of having her own personality submerged, consumed. In a true communion this would not happen; that is why absolute equality between the communicants is important. What Miriam discovers through her relationship with Amabel is that she can become close to another if the threat of "otherness" is not present. The "other," and that, by definition, would be the male, might subsume her through his assertion of superiority.

To avoid an ultimate confrontation, Miriam uses several devices to separate herself from others on the deepest level. It is possible, in fact, to view her almost compulsive concern with physical objects as one of the ways she tries to avoid contact. This interest in physical objects must not be mistaken for sensuality. Miriam's avoidance of her own physical nature and attributes is a distinguishing characteristic of her personality. Also, her own concern with physical objects must be contrasted with the obsession with things which Miriam attributes to men. Men are concerned with things because they need to have power and control. They organize their thinking into patterns that are all at one level—mechanical. The feminine involvement with things is different. It is an acceptance of all the things of the world, an appreciation of their inner essence and worth, an almost mystical sense of their individual importance. Thus one thing cannot be made superior to another. It is truly because the woman is able to hold many diverse things in her mind at one time that she does not make them into hierarchical orders of value. They all exist at the same time. But in another sense this diverse, multi-leveled apperception of reality allows one to retreat from involvement with any *one* object at a time. If they are all equally important, then they can all be equidistant from the protected, guarded center of the self.

Miriam describes physical surroundings in a manner in keeping with her philosophy of the nature of reality. A description might very well follow the movement of her eye rather than a logical organization. The following passage illustrates her kind of order:

> The West End street...grey buildings rising on either side, angles sharp against the sky...softened angles of buildings against other buildings...high moulded angles soft as crumb, with deep under-shadows...creepers fraying from balconies..strips of window blossoms across the buildings, scarlet, yellow, high up; a confusion of lavender and white pouching out along the dipping sill...a wash of green creeper up a white painted house-front...patches of shadow and bright light....Sounds of visible near things streaked and scored with broken light as they moved, led off into untraced distant sounds...chiming together. [I, 416]

She achieves here a sense of life in motion. Miriam's descriptions are rarely static. She senses constant interactions between physical objects, which actually correspond to the ceaseless movements of human beings. Another characteristic of this passage is its conglomeration of objects in a given piece of space. The objects are not organized in order of their importance, an indication of the lack of hierarchical values in the feminine consciousness. The piling up of details in a seemingly random style creates a sense of simultaneity in time. This, too, relates to Miriam's insistence on the multi-layered experience of reality that belongs to women. Miriam is aware of the richness of the scene and the scene is imprinted upon her consciousness. Yet it is separated from her self-identity. This is one of the functions of physical description in *Pilgrimage*. In fact, Miriam might even use this type of description at a point of high emotional tension in order to break away from a total confrontation with the painful situation.

Another advantage of Miriam's method of perceiving physical objects is that it allows her to fully experience the condition of "presentness." Men are always living in the future, always striving, looking ahead, unable to "be," since they are always madly becoming. Women are different; the fullest expression of the feminine consciousness is when it experiences absolute presentness. In the description of the West End street there is no past or future; the objects live in a timeless eternity. By separating her ego from them, she is able to see them as they are, not as they can be used. Miriam is able to achieve a sense of presentness even when she is recounting memories from the past. When she remembers, she does not lose consciousness of the present. The past merely becomes another one of the complex elements which make up the present moment.[19]

When Miriam is able to achieve the proper mood, when she becomes a part of the total presentness, there comes upon her a kind of mystical state. Sometimes it is brought about by an exceptionally moving visual scene, sometimes by music. For example, she listens to Emma Bergmann play the opening motif of Chopin's Fifteenth Nocturne:

> Miriam, her fatigue forgotten, slid to a featureless freedom. It seemed to her that the light with which the room was filled grew brighter and clearer. She felt that she was looking at nothing and yet was aware of the whole room like a picture in a dream. Fear left her. The human forms all round her lost their power. They grew suffused and dim....The pensive swing of the music changed to urgency and emphasis....It came nearer and nearer. It did not come from the candle-lit corner where the piano was....It came from everywhere. It carried her out of the house, out of the world. [I, 43]

Miriam's states of bliss often seem related to a release of tension, a relaxation of her almost constant defensiveness. When she refers to human forms losing their power, it almost seems as if she escapes ever having to deal with them. "Featureless freedom" is the crucial term here. While masculine consciousness is supposed to be made up of the logically arranged particles of existence, the feminine mind exists beyond all flux and change. As it is stable, it does not have to focus on any particular object; it is "featureless." It is her special sense of wonder at the presentness of everything which diffuses all objects with importance. Although they are important individually, they are even more so if they are taken

19. See Gloria Glikin's description of Richardson's use of the flashback: "The flashback, in varying degrees of length and distance, is Dorothy Richardson's chief instrument. Miriam's mind, however, is always functioning in the present and at simultaneous levels of awareness" (pp. 90–91).

in all together. This might explain the piling up of details in so many of Miriam's descriptions.[20] In the piling up, one can sense the pervading essence that binds all things:

> Miriam wondered again and again whether her companions shared this sense with her. Sometimes when they were all sitting together she longed to ask, to find out, to get some public acknowledgment of the magic that lay over everything. At times it seemed as if could they all be still for a moment—it must take shape. It was everywhere, in the food, in the fragrance rising from the opened lid of the tea-urn, in all the needful unquestioned movements, the requests, the handings and thanks, the going from room to room, the partings and assemblings. It hung about the fabrics and fittings of the house. Overwhelmingly it came in through oblongs of window giving on to stairways. [I, 158]

These experiences are solitary ones for Miriam. They permit her to be removed from other people; they allow her to experience communion, but not with people. She might wonder whether her friends feel as she does, but she makes no attempt to find out. She guards her secret life as a way of protecting her self-identity. It will not be until many years later, during her stay with the Quakers at Dimple Hill, that she will accept the need for human communion in this mystical sense. But in the meantime she holds on to physical objects as a way of maintaining being. "Being," for Miriam, represents the unchanging state which underlies all transient appearances. She believes that men are too caught up in the flux of change to accept the intuitions that arise out of a state of being. At the very heart of her conflict with Hypo lies his refusal to prefer being to becoming:

> Being versus becoming. Becoming versus being. Look after the being and the becoming will look after itself. Look after the be-

---

20. Mary Ellmann refers to the profusion of details in *Pilgrimage*: "How feminine! Objects, things, hair-pins, pince-nez, 'the profound materiality of women'" (p. 23). And Katharine Mansfield remarks: "There is Miss R., holding out her mind, as it were, and there is Life hurling objects into it as fast as she can throw. And at the appointed time Miss R. dives into its recesses and reproduces a certain number of these treasures—a pair of button boots, a night in Spring, some cycling knickers, some large, round biscuits—as many as she can pack into a book, in fact. But the pace kills" (*Novels and Novelists* (New York: Alfred A. Knopf, 1930), p. 6).

coming and the being will look after itself? Not so certain. Therefore it is certain that becoming depends upon being. Man carries
his bourne within himself and is there already, or he would not
even know that he exists. [IV, 362]

Things in themselves have an absolute "being." Perhaps that is
why they are so immensely appealing to her:

> Perhaps, in the end, things, like beloved backgrounds, are peo-
> ple. But individual objects hold the power of moving one deeply
> and immediately and always in the same way. There is no vari-
> ableness with them, neither shadow nor turning. People move
> one variously and intermittently and, in direct confrontation,
> there is nearly always a barrier. In things, even in perfectly "ordi-
> nary and commonplace" things, life is embodied. . . . After an
> interval, only after an interval—showing that there is within one-
> self something that ceaselessly contemplates "forgotten" things
> —a fragment of stone, even a photograph, has the power of
> making one enter a kingdom one hardly knew one possessed.
> Whose riches increase, even though they are inanimate. But, if
> greatly loved, are they inanimate? They are destructible. Perhaps
> the secret is there. People cannot be destroyed. Things can. From
> the moment they come into being, they are at the mercy of acci-
> dent. [IV, 368]

Things here are one-dimensional. They call forth the same responses each time they are experienced. This makes any experience with them predictable. Such a condition is absent in
relationships with people. And certainly the desire for absoluteness marks many of Miriam's insecurities. It is often easier to
retreat from people altogether than to face the possibility of their
disagreement, their lack of feeling for what one is feeling, their
differing perceptions about a situation. And when it comes to relationships bound up with a great amount of risk (any of those
with men would qualify here), especially risk to the impenetrabil-
ity of the ego, then it is better perhaps to forgo them in favor of
a kind of mystical communion with nature and the things of this
world. There, one's responses are certain. They come from only
one side. They are always the same and can be controlled, because
only one partner in the relationship has any power of will.

Even though Miriam is able to control her reactions to "a fragment of stone," since she does not have to fear the stone's reaction to her, she cannot control the reactions of a man. Thus it is precisely in the areas of sex that she has so much trouble. It was easier when she had to deal with Amabel. There she could work with responses similar to her own. It was an identity of selves—a narcissistic kind of dual mind. But she cannot accept the affronts of an alien consciousness, and for Miriam the male consciousness seems totally alien. The demands for submission, loss of identity, loss of self, called for in sexual relationships are unbearable for her. That is why she so often retreats into reverie while she is experiencing sexual contact. She can remove herself from her partner if she lets her mind move away during physical contact. Miriam's trips are always lonely ones. The only description of a state of high emotional excitement owing to physical contact with a man, in all of *Pilgrimage*, occurs when Miriam is first kissed by Michael Shatov. And there it is obvious that her ecstatic state has little to do with the presence of that particular man. His kiss sends her off on a lonely journey within her mind. The scenes with Hypo, by comparison, are marked by self-consciousness and criticism of her partner. The actual consummation of their attraction is not even described; it is merely hinted at. During the scenes when they come close to sexual intercourse, Miriam is always put off by some incongruous characteristic in Hypo, either physical or mental. With Densley, no physical contact takes place. And instead of isolation during physical contact, she experiences isolation through thinking out her future dreams of marriage separately from him. Miriam has remained solitary and separated throughout all her relationships with men.

Instead of developing the close human contact necessary for a complete sexual relationship, Miriam usually remains involved with her own self-development. Her moods of mystical absorption allow her to maintain individual identity. Her insistence upon "being" as opposed to "becoming" as the center of the feminine consciousness permits her to accept the self as a contained and basically unchanging center which is not affected by contacts with others. It is an abstract, isolated entity. Yet, in a sense, this whole concept of "being" runs counter to the purpose and plan of the novel and the telling of those innumerable experiences throughout those interminable pages. If "being" is a static thing, it might be revealed in a very short form. A single symbolic incident would probably be enough. Symbolism of a vague sort can be discovered in *Pilgrimage*, but it is not a distinguishing characteristic of it. Instead, the novel is discursive. Dorothy Richardson tries to capture the flowing, volatile character of Miriam's mind through endless variations which are produced by the millions of present moments that make up an individual's mental life. The whole process is described as a "pilgrimage," and so it does seem to be. At one point Miriam insists: "I must create my life. Life is creation. Self and circumstances the raw material" (III, 508).

This creation seems to be a form of "becoming"—changing, altering through the subtle pressures of external impressions and one's reflections upon them. Miriam learns and grows and changes, and seems to be in search of that "being" which she asserts exists without the searching. The completing irony of the whole process is that this "being" Miriam seeks, she believes to be a natural part of the feminine consciousness. But somehow it cannot be sought through accepting the sexual nature of femininity at all. Miriam insists upon its femininity yet refuses to put "femininity" into its natural, physical setting. This femininity is a femininity of mind, and Miriam does not seem to have it in herself with any great sense of surety. The "feminine consciousness" remains strangely abstract and separated from its normal connection with the body—which is the basic source of femininity—and its fullest revelation is to be a state of mystical awareness and communion with God. This is a lonely and asexual achievement of "being."

Two

May Sinclair

ALTHOUGH at one time the name of May Sinclair (1865?–1946) was linked with that of Dorothy Richardson as an innovator in the stream-of-consciousness mode, her name is now unfamiliar even to serious students of English literature. She was not one of the giants of modern literature, surely not a Joyce or a Woolf, nor was she a true inventor of fictional forms, like Dorothy Richardson. Instead, she wrote competent novels about many subjects during a long and successful career, and it is as a popularizer of themes and techniques which belonged to the avant-garde that she maintains her interest and usefulness for this study of the feminine consciousness.

Her novels are carefully constructed, clearly written, and contain only that amount of technical innovation which her readers could easily handle (and think of themselves as "modern" at the same time). She worked into her books concepts from psychology which were new and disturbing to those readers. She used Freudian concepts before any other English novelist, and notions such as repression, suppression, dream symbolism, and the like fill her novels.[1] In addition, she was a serious scholar widely read in biol-

---

1. For discussion of Freudian influences, see Dorothy Brewster and Angus Burrell, *Dead Reckonings in Fiction* (New York: Longmans, Green, 1924), pp. 176–254; Gerald Bullett, *Modern English Fiction* (London: Herbert Jenkins,

ogy, psychology, and philosophy and concerned with such social questions as the war in Europe and feminism.

As a student of literature she produced criticism of considerable sensitivity and awareness, and she had the ability to put what she had learned in other fields immediately into a fictional form. The very term "stream of consciousness" belongs to May Sinclair. Actually William James used it first in discussing the workings of the mind, but she was the first to apply it to the content of a work of fiction—to give it a literary connotation. It happened in April, 1918, when she wrote an article called "The Novels of Dorothy Richardson."[2] Thus she was one of Dorothy Richardson's first admirers and defenders. She was fully aware of what Dorothy Richardson was trying to do; she approved of it. The whole idea seemed to appeal to her subjectively, for very soon after that she published her own exposition of the "stream" in *Mary Olivier* (1919).[3]

The connection between May Sinclair and Dorothy Richardson is obvious, yet it would do May Sinclair an injustice to begin an analysis of the feminine consciousness in her work as if it were something that appeared only after she became acquainted with *Pilgrimage*.[4] In a sense, her stream-of-consciousness novel was the outgrowth of her own ideas and development as a novelist. It appears that her reading of *Pointed Roofs* (1915) exploded her

---

1926), pp. 99–102; Walter L. Myers, *The Later Realism* (Chicago: University of Chicago Press, 1927), pp. 45–56; Frank Swinnerton, *The Georgian Scene* (New York: Farrar & Rinehart, 1934), pp. 385–86; and William York Tindall, *Forces in Modern British Literature* (New York: Vintage Books, 1956), pp. 218–19. See also T. E. M. Boll, "On the May Sinclair Collection," *Library Chronicle*, 27 (Winter, 1961), 2. Boll argues that May Sinclair has been misplaced as a Freudian, that her concepts are really Jungian. He has written the only biography of May Sinclair, which appeared just after my own manuscript was completed: T. E. M. Boll, *Miss May Sinclair, Novelist: A Biographical and Critical Introduction* (Rutherford, N.J.: Fairleigh Dickinson University Press, 1973).

2. May Sinclair, "The Novels of Dorothy Richardson," *Little Review*, 4 (Apr., 1918), 3–11.

3. May Sinclair, *Mary Olivier: A Life* (New York: Macmillan, 1919).

4. Among the critics who discuss the similarities between May Sinclair and Dorothy Richardson are Myers, p. 86; R. Brimley Johnson, *Some Contemporary Novelists (Women)* (London: Leonard Parsons, 1920), p. 41; C. A. Dawson-Scott in *Bookman* (Nov., 1920), p. 248; and Babette Deutsch in *Dial*, 67 (Nov. 15, 1919), 441.

old patterns and preconceptions. She recognized something in Dorothy Richardson which was also within herself, and she knew enough to act upon that recognition, for by 1919 she had already enjoyed a long and prolific career as a novelist.[5]

To tell the truth, however, May Sinclair's stream is more a platonic ideal than a specific and particular stream like the one which exists in its totality within the pages of *Pilgrimage*. Miriam Henderson, while basically a creature of mind with only peripheral awareness of body, pursues reality nonetheless through sexuality and tries to discover true freedom of action as well as thought. Her search is revealed through an examination of the contents of her mind, and it is a mind seemingly without boundaries. If one reflects on the stream image in relation to Dorothy Richardson's work, the metaphor might connote a great river, with deltas and sloughs and marshes and meandering brooks, all flowing from a huge, still, and peaceful lake. It contains few rushing torrents or waterfalls, and rarely does a flood overflow its banks. In contrast, May Sinclair provides Mary Olivier with a stream that is quite orderly, a mountain brook, cold, icy, clear, exposing the smooth distinct stones underneath. It moves from its glacial lake and flows regularly down to the sea. It has no tributaries, no marshes, and no mud.

Several years after *Mary Olivier*, in one of her last three novels, *Far End* (1926),[6] May Sinclair put the theory behind her conception of "stream of consciousness" fiction into a dramatic form, using ideas and even exact phrases from her essay on the novels of Dorothy Richardson. It is a fine example of the way she transposes ideas from other sources into her fiction. Moreover, it expresses most clearly, and in extremely simple terms, the essence of a rather abstruse literary method. In the novel Christopher Vivart, a prominent novelist, explains his new work, *Peter Harden*, to a visiting critic:

5. May Sinclair was an extremely prolific writer. By the time she stopped writing in 1931, she had published twenty-two novels, three books of poetry, several short story collections, two philosophical treatises, a journal of her experience as an ambulance driver in World War I, a literary biography of the Brontës, as well as many miscellaneous pieces of criticism and philosophy.

6. May Sinclair, *Far End* (New York: Macmillan, 1926).

"I'm eliminating God Almighty, the all-wise, all-seeing author."

"Eliminating yourself. How do you manage that? You tell the story. You make things happen."

"Only as they happen in Peter Harden's consciousness. I don't stand outside, I work from the inside out. . . ."

"Then none of the other characters," said Burton, "can be properly drawn."

"They are just as properly drawn as the characters we meet in our own lives. We have nothing to go on but our own consciousness of other people. . . . They're just as real as people in anybody's world. In fact they should be more real than God Almighty's people because they're appearing in their natural setting of a mind. Peter's consciousness is as good as anybody else's consciousness. Of course there's no absolute certainty about them, but then there's no absolute certainty about the people that we know. . . . Nobody interferes with Peter's reality. There's no author running about arranging and analysing and explaining and representing. It's presentation, not representation, all the time. There's nothing but the stream of Peter's consciousness. The book *is* a stream of consciousness, going on and on; it's life itself going on and on."

". . . And what have you gained, you, more than God Almighty, when you've got it?"

"Can't you see? I gain a unity which is a unity of form, and more than a unity of form, a unity of substance, an intense reality where no film or shadow of anything extraneous comes between. I present a world of one consciousness, undivided and undefiled, a world which is everybody's world. You can't stand outside of your own consciousness, and the nearer you get down to one consciousness the nearer you'll be to reality. That's all." [*Far End,* pp. 81–84]

May Sinclair's treatment of Mary's stream of consciousness is not an endless outpouring of the endless perceptions and reflections which may occur in any given interval of time. Her stream is merely the *imitation* of a stream, not a stream at all.[7] And that stream is presented through a use of point of view slightly different from the omniscient narrator of *Pilgrimage,* who was able to ob-

7. Abel Chevalley, *The Modern English Novel,* tr. Ben Ray Redman (New York: Alfred A. Knopf, 1930), p. 206, defined May Sinclair's technique in *Mary Olivier* as "impressionism, *pointillisme.*"

serve each slight movement of Miriam's mind. There is an omniscient narrator for Mary also, but it is not an impersonal one; it is Mary herself. Usually this narrator describes the thoughts in Mary's mind through the conventional third-person "she." This is where the writer Mary, looking at her own life from a great distance in time or feeling, separates herself from the thoughts of the character Mary. This is possible because one is always able, even though it is difficult, to view oneself as another person. But when the omniscient narrator gets closer and closer to identification with the character Mary, the pronouns change. Thus she speaks to that other self. "You," she calls it. And then, almost with a startling-seeming inconsistency, she switches to "I." In these passages she gives us the mind itself, free from any interpretation.

The shift from third to second person is sometimes confusing, as in the following example: "Mamma took her in her lap. She lowered her head to you, holding it straight and still, ready to pounce if you said the wrong thing" (p. 28). Here we have an indication that the perspective is shifting away from the distant Mary to her own reflections. She is telling herself what was going on in herself. The narrator, then, is also "you," but the "you" who looks back.

Occasionally the time of the point of view changes. For instance, after recounting an event in which Mary took part as a child, the adult Mary (and this time it is the adult narrator Mary) speaks in an aside. She tells the reader something that the child Mary (who was undergoing the experience) could never have felt: "Darling Mamma. She had taken them because she thought they would like it" (p. 57). This is the mature Mary speaking as she looks back and understands now what her mother was really trying to do then.

It is instructive to keep in mind the beginning of Joyce's *A Portrait of the Artist as a Young Man* while considering the opening of *Mary Olivier*. The evolution of a woman's mind is illustrated by key memories and events. May Sinclair begins with infancy, as did Joyce, but she does not try to capture the sentence structure and diction of the infant mind. Instead, it is a re-creation through memory: "In the dark you could go tip-finger along the slender, lashing flourishes of the ironwork" (p. 1). The preceding sentence is a typical one. It uses the second-person point of view, and it shows the infant mind focused on physical objects. The early sections of the novel have the choppy, disconnected feeling of early memories, but they are not chosen at random. They form short sections which reveal a complete incident, an important step in the development of Mary's mind and emotions. Each incident captures the *quality* of Mary's mind at that stage of her growth, but it does not necessarily give us the mind itself. The quality of thinking at the specific time—such as the concentration on physical objects in the memories of infancy—seems to influence the selection.

Mary's memories are usually explained by direct sentences which describe an incident in her life and her feelings about that incident at the time. These sections do not reveal Mary's stream of consciousness; rather, they are reports from Mary the omniscient narrator. But usually within them Mary brings about a sense of realization of her consciousness at the time. After the narrator describes a heated discussion between Mary and her parents and aunt, she gives us next Mary's reaction to the event immediately after it took place. But she does not give us Mary's feelings *at the moment* of its taking place. Instead, we see Mary in her bed after it is over, and then the images in her mind tumble out: "The scene rose again and swam before her and fell to pieces. Ideas—echoes—images. Religion—the truth of God. Her father's voice booming over the table. Aunt Lavvy's voice, breaking—breaking. A pile of stripped chicken bones on her father's plate" (p. 107). The images are set apart by dashes, as if to indicate that they appeared almost simultaneously in Mary's mind. This is an interesting treatment of a memory of a memory. The memory that the adult Mary has of the dinner argument is described in narrative form with the events occurring in the time sequence in which they actually took place, with the exception of the inevitable distortions which cause condensation in any memory of an event long past. But she also gives us the memory which occurred immediately after the event. And this memory is totally disjointed. Through the forceful energy created by emotions, the more immediate memory is a jumble of superimposed images. The importance of the event is encapsulated in concrete forms. And their connections with each other are not based on sequential time. The sentence structure—incomplete sentences with only a subjective clause—then fits the level of consciousness which it is supposed to represent.

Sometimes May Sinclair describes Mary's consciousness in a manner reminiscent of Dorothy Richardson's treatment of Miriam Henderson. Coincidentally, one of the most obvious examples occurs in a description of an experience similar to one of Miriam's in *Pointed Roofs*: traveling to school with her father. May Sinclair uses here a more personal version of the third-person narrator:

> She was shut up with Papa, tight, in the narrow cab that smelt of the mews. Papa, sitting slantways, nearly filled the cab. He was quiet and sad, almost as if he were sorry she was going.

Note how the passage begins in the third person but moves next, in the following paragraph, to the second:

> His sadness and quietness fascinated her. He had a mysterious, wonderful, secret life going on in him. Funny you should think of it for the first time in the cab. Supposing you stroked his hand. Better not. He mightn't like it.
>
> Not forty minutes from Liverpool Street to Victoria. If only cabs didn't smell so.

By the time she reaches the last paragraph of this short section (it is set apart from the rest of the chapter by a subheading, a small roman numeral), the point of view seems immediate, not a memory at all. It is the direct consciousness of Mary as an adolescent. It is in the present tense. A similar and also more intensified shift in time as well as point of view occurs in the following section (ii, of Chapter XVIII):

> The small, ugly houses streamed past, backs turned to the rain, stuck together, rushing rushing in from the country.
>
> Grey streets, trying to cut across the stream, getting nowhere, carried past sideways on.
>
> Don't look at the houses. Shut your eyes and remember.

Her father's hand on her shoulder. His face, at the carriage window, looking for her. A girl moving back, pushing her to it. "Papa!"

Why hadn't she loved him all the time? Why hadn't she liked his beard? His nice, brown, silky beard. His poor beard.

Mamma's face, in the hall, breaking up suddenly. Her tears in your mouth. Her arms, crushing you. Mamma's face at the dining-room window. Tears, pricking, cutting your eyelids. Blink them back before the girls see them. Don't think of Mamma.

The Thames. Barking Creek goes into the Thames and the Roding goes into Barking Creek. Yesterday, the last walk with Roddy across Barking Flats to the river, over. . . . [Pp. 135–36]

Only the first verb in the passage, "streamed past," reminds us that the narrator is looking back. The other verbs are in the present tense as they describe Mary's immediate perceptions.

Another feature of May Sinclair's treatment of Mary's stream of consciousness is her depiction of the mind's involvement with itself. At several points in the novel Mary thinks about thinking. For instance, eleven-year-old Mary considers an abstract statement: "Nobody has any innate ideas. Children and savages and idiots haven't any, so grown-up people can't have, Mr. Locke says. But how did he know? You might have them and forget about them, and only remember again after you were grown up" (p. 82). As the preceding reveals, when the narrator wants to show Mary thinking about an issue, she often gives us the sequence of her thought as it probably occurred, in order to show what level of maturity Mary's thinking had reached. In this case Mary is not yet an adolescent, and her thoughts about abstract ideas contain remnants of childish associations. "Mr. Locke says" appearing at the end of the sentence gives it the sing-song quality of childish conversations. It also makes Locke a person to be reckoned with, like a teacher or a parent.

Once in a while, the direct representation of thought processes involves the preoccupation of mind with language. Mary often thinks about words and lets her mind spin out fanciful associations as she plays with them:

"Don't look like that," her mother said, "as if your wits were wool-gathering."

"Wool?" She could see herself smiling at her mother, disagreeably.

Wool-gathering. Gathering wool. The room was full of wool; wool flying about; hanging in the air and choking you. Clogging your mind. Old grey wool out of pew cushions that people had sat on for centuries, full of dirt.

Wool, spun out, wound round you, woven in a net. You were tangled and strangled in a net of unclean wool. They caught you in it when you were a baby a month old. Mamma, Papa and Uncle Victor. You would have to cut and tug and kick and fight your way out. They were caught in it themselves, and they couldn't get out. They didn't want to get out. The wool stopped their minds working. They hated it when their minds worked, when anybody's mind worked. Aunt Lavvy's—yours. [P. 113]

This use of a significant image allows all sorts of associations to occur in Mary's mind. At first the image is literal—wool. And she sees it flying all about her. Then the psychological significance of wool occurs to her. And that is neatly related to her mother's attempted dominance over her thinking. Her mother said the word originally, and in so doing interfered with Mary's freedom, so Mary gets back at her through imagining how her mother would like to bind her up in it to keep her mind from growing. She even extends the image to the larger issue of environmental determinism. She is aware of the net that has held her since infancy, "a net of unclean wool." It is through the use of such images that Mary often penetrates through to an understanding of herself.

Another characteristic of Mary's thinking is her personalization of ideas. Abstractions become concrete. As a child, she thinks about numbers, for example:

At night when you lay on your back in the dark you thought about being born and about arithmetic and God. The sacred number three went into eighteen sixty-nine and didn't come out again; so did seven. She liked numbers that fitted like that with no loose ends left over. Mr. Sippett said there were things you could do with the loose ends of numbers to make them fit. That was fractions. Supposing there was somewhere in the world a number that simply wouldn't fit? Mr. Sippett said there was no such number. But queer things happened. You were seven years old, yet you had had eight birthdays. [P. 45]

Or another time she visualizes "the French verbs, grey, slender as little verses on the page" (p. 141). Or she takes cold facts from reading, from history or literature, and fleshes them out, like these gods and goddesses from mythology: "They cared for all the things you liked best: trees and animals and poetry and music and running races and playing games" (pp. 78–79).

And over and over again words themselves take on lives of their own. Words have sacred significance beyond what they symbolize. They are concrete; they are things. Like the numbers which needed to fit in order to make her feel at ease, words too must be right, must "fit." For these disturbances over numbers or words, or the visual constructs they become for her, reveal how closely she ties all ideas to her own feelings. And it is this emotionality, more than anything else, this relating of ideas to feelings and then being unable to separate them again, which keeps Mary from the independence she desires.

II   Mary Olivier's "feminine consciousness" resembles in
some respects the characteristics Dorothy Richardson combined in her portrayal of Miriam Henderson. Mary is like Miriam in that she is ambivalent about her role as a woman, intellectual, rebellious, and mystical. But all of these qualities are related to a tremendous sense of oppression and restriction in the case of Mary Olivier. Mary certainly has the inquisitive spirit that marks Miriam Henderson, but May Sinclair shows us the development of her feminine consciousness through a different method and out of a quite different body of beliefs about the nature of human emotions.

She came to the writing of fiction from a background heavy with the burden of her extensive reading in philosophy and biology. This was the nineteenth-century mixture of science and sociology, with its notions of the survival of the fittest, the respect for power, and the determinism of organic development carried over into the realms of philosophy and politics. Her familiarity with Darwin and Herbert Spencer is evidenced in the program of reading she makes Mary Olivier undertake. The issue of heredity —especially the inheritance of mental illness—concerned her. It was perhaps that concern which would eventually lead her away from theories of biological inheritance of mental disorder to Freudian conceptions of illness caused by repression. She was a popular writer who attempted to absorb and communicate in simple terms the currents of scholarship around her—philosophy, psychology, and metaphysics—so it is not surprising to find them all reflected in her fiction. In fact, her very notion of the feminine consciousness grows out of these varied sources.

From the biological sciences she took the notion of determinism. If one starts with the concept of a seed or germ containing all the components of the full-grown plant or animal, one discovers an inherent determinism there. If one adds to it the necessity provided by environmental conditions, the human being is not left with much "freedom." And then, if one compounds these difficulties by adding to them the inescapable conflicts built into the race by those basic urges and fears so imaginatively described by Freud, the construct of "character" which emerges reflects these overpowering external controls. Thus it is not surprising to discover how much more closely and tightly controlled is Mary's consciousness compared with Miriam Henderson's.

Since May Sinclair brings that whole body of deterministic theories to bear upon Mary, her life is thus circumscribed by environment and heredity, and these enforced limitations are described as inescapable. The struggle for power may take place on the most personal levels as well as social ones, especially within the family, with all those Oedipal difficulties arising during child-raising, the struggle for dominance within one's sexual identity, the establishing of sexual roles. Thus Mary Olivier struggles desperately against her mother's domination. The woman restricts Mary's creativity and expressions of sexuality, forces her to give up her own life in order to devote it to hers. But this is what she has to do; her character is also determined. Consequently Mary does not hate her mother, although she is aware of the woman's horrifying power over her. Mary also realizes that she can do nothing about it; her fate is out of her own hands.

As a result Mary never achieves the freedom in her daily life that is so remarkable with Miriam. Miriam leaves—actually is forced to leave her family—and in so doing becomes independent and strong. Mary is forced to stay and gradually gives up the strong-willed passions of her youth as she cares for her domineering mother and retreats further into the life of the mind. Her one chance for fulfillment comes when she nears middle age and falls in love with a famous writer who returns her love and wishes to marry her. But she insists she cannot marry Richard because she will not leave her mother. Conditions force Mary's actions; Miriam always insisted upon changing conditions. Thus on some levels *Mary Olivier* is a protest novel. That is, it protests the conditions which force talented and intelligent women to live empty lives. This social sense is quite different from the intensely personal "pilgrimage" Dorothy Richardson was describing.

After all, Dorothy Richardson was in pursuit of the freedom of the consciousness rather than the limitations which are placed upon it. She was looking at the innumerable perceptions which change from moment to moment, at life seen in the concrete, in the particularities, never in terms of totalities; she believed this was the essence of the feminine consciousness. May Sinclair, on the other hand, was not existentialistic. Her writings in philosophy were about idealism. She was influenced by Freudian and Jungian studies in symbolism; consequently she was interested in the recurring nature of experience as it is revealed through symbols. Therefore, although *Mary Olivier* is also a deeply personal novel, its more detached point of view and more organically unified construction tend to symbolize both character and conditions and give them larger implications. The pressures of heredity and environment and natural drives seem to work toward the creation of a type rather than an individual. One might say that May Sinclair's characters, in general, do not have the amorphous, erratic, idiosyncratic personalities which are so evident in *Pilgrimage*.

Therefore, if one is to analyze the feminine consciousness in *Mary Olivier*, one must be aware that it is to be interpreted generally as well as specifically. Miriam Henderson is Miriam Henderson at every minute and every second that she lives for us; she is never "Woman" or even "Intellectual Woman." Mary is a *type* of woman as well as a particular woman.[8] But what seems to make this novel stronger than so many of her others is the precision of May Sinclair's characterization of Mary. Some critics attribute this to the autobiographical nature of the work, insisting that May Sinclair was working out through Mary her own life and problems —a question not at issue here. Autobiographical or not, Mary Olivier has the power of a realized character.

In 1897 May Sinclair asserted that the three "dominating myths of modernity" were "Custom, Circumstance and Heredity,"[9] and throughout her fiction one can see these "myths" in operation. They precede her interest in consciousness itself, but they are eventually used to modify and direct her concept of consciousness when it appears. What is relevant to the purpose of this study is how these concepts from Naturalism are involved with the feminine character and the behavior of women in her novels. There sexual role seems to determine a woman's direction in life, and this is treated as a fact of nature by May Sinclair, as the following passage from an essay written in 1912 indicates: "That only one sex should pay is Nature's economy. It happened to be woman. And you are bound, on a one-sided arrangement of this sort, to get, in sexual relations, a profounder feeling, a finer moral splendour, a superior sex virtue in the sex that pays."[10]

In the relations between men and women, May Sinclair implies, there are always dominant and subordinate roles. The woman has of course been the one to give in, to give up her own claims for autonomy in favor of her husband. By sticking closely to the biological interpretation of woman's role, May Sinclair seems to

8. This type-casting is even more obvious and assured in *Life and Death of Harriett Frean* (New York: Macmillan, 1922).

9. May Sinclair, *Audrey Craven* (1897; reprinted, New York: Henry Holt, 1907), p. 4.

10. May Sinclair, "A Defence of Men," *English Review*, 11 (July, 1912), 559.

be saying here that self-sacrifice on the part of the woman is inevitable, and that this self-sacrifice gives the woman the moral edge.

In nearly every one of May Sinclair's novels there is a character who gives up the chance for self-fulfillment in order to help someone else. Although this is a man in a few cases,[11] it is usually a woman who "pays," as it is the determinism of sex which complicates the issue of power. Thus one finds women in her novels who "pay" by subordinating themselves to domineering and insensitive husbands,[12] women who "pay" by giving in to their sexual drives outside marriage and are punished by society,[13] and women who go further and even remove themselves from sexual relations altogether, in order to realize a more "noble" ideal, giving up a lover to someone else, a sister or friend.[14] But nobody sacrifices so much of herself as Mary Olivier, for she has more energy and talent and sensitivity than any of the other characters. In fact, her intelligence exemplifies what May Sinclair described as nature's tendency "to produce better and better, and larger and more complex brains, in response to larger and more complex needs, and on the upward lines of her own evolution."[15] Mary is one of a new breed of "doubly vital women," with superior mental and physical capabilities, so that in terms of natural selection, her refusal to marry is unfortunate indeed.

III   Mary Olivier's "feminine consciousness" grows partly out
        of how she is treated because of her sex and how her sexual

11. Mary Olivier's brothers also sacrifice themselves for their mother. Other male characters who perform noble acts of self-sacrifice in Sinclair's novels are Ranny in *The Combined Maze* (New York: Macaulay, 1913); *Arnold Waterlow* (New York: Macmillan, 1924); and *History of Anthony Waring* (New York: Macmillan, 1927).

12. See May Sinclair, *The Tysons* (New York: Grosset & Dunlap, 1906) and *The Judgment of Eve* (New York: Harper, 1908). The latter work, a novella, outlines the career of a woman destroyed by too many childbirths, and implies that a woman has no power in controlling the sexual drives of her husband.

13. The best example is Kitty Tailleur in May Sinclair, *The Immortal Moment: The Story of Kitty Tailleur* (New York: Doubleday, Page, 1908).

14. Harriet Frean gives up her lover to her best friend, and Gwendolyn gives up hers to her own sister in *The Three Sisters* (New York: Macmillan, 1914).

15. May Sinclair, *Feminism* (London: Women Writers' Suffrage League, 1912), p. 23.

feelings influence her thinking. The only girl in a family with three sons, her first conflicts grow out of her jealousy over her mother's preference for the boys, especially the eldest, Mark. She longs for her mother's love and is tormented by its absence all her life. As a child she builds a tower out of bricks, but her mother is too busy looking at her brother's snowman to pay attention:

> Something swelled up, hot and tight, in Mary's body and in her face. She had a big bursting face and a big bursting body. She struck the tower, and it fell down. Her violence made her feel light and small again and happy.
> "Where's the tower, Mary?" said Mamma.
> "There isn't any tar. I've knocked it down. It was a nashty tar."
> [P.10]

Mary's anger at her mother, and the association of that anger with the destruction of a masculine symbol (May Sinclair uses obviously "Freudian" symbols frequently), are what make the passage significant. But one must also keep in mind that the incident figures in Mary's memory years after the event. She has singled out this scene and recorded it, an indication that she probably understands how it has influenced her. The scene reveals how Mary learns to minimize, and in fact to turn against, her own accomplishments. She is at the stage where she must give up her active strivings (Freud would say that she must give up her masculine strivings for her mother—and in this case the tower is perfectly fitting as a symbol), but the giving up is accompanied by hostile feelings toward the mother. Mary has to accept that she is a girl and, since she is a girl, that she comes last in her mother's affections. She also learns that she will receive attention only negatively, through contrary actions rather than through her creativity.

Not only is Mary jealous here of her mother's interest in the boys, especially Mark, but that very jealousy is turned inside out and allows her to feel passionate feelings for the very person who has caused her the most grief. She falls in love with her brother Mark and thus identifies herself with her mother, who loves him more than anyone. Here Mary deviates from the classic Freudian pattern, where the love for the mother is turned to the father.

Since Mary's father is so ineffective (he later becomes an alcoholic), neither the mother nor Mary can focus their sexual desires upon him, and so the brothers take his place. In fact, the poor man frequently reveals his jealousy of his sons and remarks upon his wife's preference for them over himself and Mary.

Once when Mary was a very small child she said, "I shall paint pictures and play the piano and ride in a circus. I shall go out to the countries where the sand is and tame zebras; and I shall marry Mark and have thirteen children with blue eyes . . ." (p. 60). Mary not only wants to assume her mother's role and "marry" her brother (since her mother did, at least unconsciously, carry out this kind of Oedipal relationship with her son), but since she wants her mother's love so badly she also wants to *be* her brother. Naturally, this is what produces the tremendous conflict she feels within her feminine role. During much of her girlhood and adolescence she struggles against being a girl, and a continuous battle with her mother over her rebellion is the result: " 'Why do you look at me so kindly when I'm sewing?' 'Because I like to see you behaving like a little girl, instead of tearing about and trying to do what boys do' " (p. 70).

As a child, "trying to do what boys do" means excessive physical activity—daredevil feats like hanging out of the window, or jumping off a roof, or running carelessly in the fields. Later, in adolescence, it means studying, reading, thinking out ideas. "Men . . . are *not* interested in little bookworms," her mother tells her (p. 88).

Mary's role confusion is most obvious when she is with other girls. She does not know whether to approach them as one of them or as a different order of being. She can look at them with longing—"The queer she-things had a wonderful, mysterious life you couldn't touch" (p. 138)—but she does not see herself as sharing in that life. On the other hand, Mary also has strongly maternal desires. Yet ironically, her mother makes her ashamed of them because they reflect an interest in sex. Mary plays with baby clothes and has an imaginary group of babies to care for. When her mother discovers her playing with these "babies," she

becomes furious and reacts as if she had discovered Mary doing
something shameful:

> "That was all very well when you were a little thing. But a great
> girl of twelve—You ought to be ashamed of yourself."
>
> Mamma had gone. She had taken away the babyclothes. Mary
> lay face downwards on her bed.
>
> Shame burned through her body like fire. Hot tears scalded
> her eyelids. She thought: "How was I to know you mustn't have
> babies?" Still, she couldn't give them all up. She *must* keep Isabel
> and the red-haired baby. [Pp. 85–86]

As she matures, the idea of babies continues to produce an emotional reaction:

> A sharp and tender pang went through her. It was like desire;
> like the feeling you had when you thought of babies; painful and
> at the same time delicious. [P. 263]

And a much later memory serves to tie together the desire for
babies with the one for her brother Mark:

> Sometimes the door stood open. She would go in. She would
> go up the stairs and down the passages, trying to find the school-
> room. She would know that Mark was in the schoolroom. But she
> could never find it. She never saw Mark. The passages led through
> empty, grey-lit rooms to the bottom of the kitchen stairs, and she
> would find a dead baby lying among the boots and shoes in the
> cat's cupboard.
>
> Autumn and winter passed. She was thirty-two. [Pp. 310–11]

Mary's lack of sexual realization, while primarily related to this
confusion in role—love-hate for her mother, desire for her brother
—is also connected with the fear of sex itself, transmitted to her
through her mother's Victorian views, and more deeply through
her belief that she has inherited her Aunt Charlotte's weakness.
Any attempt at asserting her feminine desires is thwarted when
her mother insists on comparing them with Aunt Charlotte's
warped version of those desires. Thus the image of the dead baby
in the closet is also connected with a dream that Mary had during

the same night her aunt went permanently insane. Aunt Charlotte symbolizes sexual repression, but she is also a symbol of fear for Mary; Mary is afraid that she will end up like her aunt, that within herself is this same frightening drive for sex, this uncontrolled passion which becomes a sickness. Mary's fears here relate clearly to the theme of determinism and provide the most obvious example of that theme in *Mary Olivier.*

It is instructive in this regard to notice how Mary reflects upon an outrageous thing that Aunt Charlotte did to her when she was a child. Mary only records the external actions, not her childish feelings about their importance:

> Aunt Charlotte put her hand deep down in her pocket and brought out a little parcel wrapped in white paper. She whispered:
> "If I give you something to keep, will you promise not to show it to anybody and not to tell?"
> Mary promised.
> Inside the paper wrapper there was a match-box, and inside the match-box there was a china doll no bigger than your finger. It had blue eyes and black hair and no clothes on. Aunt Charlotte held it in her hand and smiled at it.
> "That's Aunt Charlotte's little baby," she said. "I'm going to be married and I shan't want it any more."
> "There—take it, and cover it up, quick!"
> Mamma had come out of the dining-room. She shut the door behind her.
> "What have you given to Mary?" she said.
> "Butter-Scotch," said Aunt Charlotte. [P. 37]

Mary does not comment upon this event in any conscious manner. Instead, immediately following in the next chapter, it appears to make its impression on her unconscious through its revelation in her dream. The dream allows for the penetration to a much deeper level of consciousness than would be possible merely through Mary's memory of the event.

> ... That night she dreamed that she saw Aunt Charlotte standing at the foot of the kitchen stairs taking off her clothes and wrapping them in white paper; first, her black lace shawl; then her chemise. She stood up without anything on. Her body was pol-

ished and shining like an enormous white china doll. She lowered her head and pointed at you with her eyes.

When you opened the stair cupboard door to catch the opossum, you found a white china doll lying in it, no bigger than your finger. That was Aunt Charlotte.

In the dream there was no break between the end and the beginning. But when she remembered it afterwards it split into two pieces with a dark gap between. She knew she had only dreamed about the cupboard; but Aunt Charlotte at the foot of the stairs was so clear and solid that she thought she had really seen her. [Pp. 37–38]

Years later, on the night when Aunt Charlotte went totally mad, the following occurred:

She had dreamed that she saw Aunt Charlotte standing at the foot of the basement stairs, by the cat's cupboard where the kittens were born, taking her clothes off and hiding them. She had seen that before. When she was six years old. She didn't know whether she had been dreaming about something that had really happened, or about a dream. Only, this time, she saw Aunt Charlotte open her mouth and scream. The scream woke her. [P. 152]

Mary's interpretation of her own inner development includes not only memories of experiences, but memories of experiences on a deeper level of consciousness, a level which is only discernible through dreams and fantasies. Here May Sinclair's familiarity with Freudian case histories and dream analyses makes its presence felt. She gives us a layer of consciousness that is available only through symbols and cannot be expressed directly as thoughts. In her earlier novels May Sinclair used dreams as the only way in which consciousness is presented directly to the reader.[16] In *Mary Olivier* and the novels which follow, she uses dreams also to circumvent improprieties, for after all May Sinclair may be considered a very proper novelist.[17]

16. As early as 1908 in *The Immortal Moment*, May Sinclair used a dream to demonstrate the turning point in a character's life. There the dream gave Kitty the answer to her problems: to kill herself.

17. In *The Romantic* (New York: Macmillan, 1920), May Sinclair uses a dream to explain a character's impotence. It is filled with falling towers, crumbling villages, rivers, and assorted other Freudian symbols.

IV   Mary's sexual life is thwarted by all of these inhibitions: role confusion, love for her brother, obsession with her mother, and fear of an insanity related to sexuality. Later her fiance gives her up when she grows into a rather graceless, scholarly woman. She is unable to behave like the conventional "good" girl, and she cannot become a free, emancipated woman because it would hurt her mother. She remains then at home, as years go by, developing the "masculine" side of her self, her intellect. She creates: writes poetry, philosophical articles. She is aware of how her creativity results from suppression of her sexual drives: "The poem would be made up of many poems. It would last a long time, through the winter and on into the spring. As long as it lasted she would be happy. She would be free from the restlessness and the endless idiotic reverie of desire" (p. 234).

Nevertheless, May Sinclair does not see Mary's life as a wasted one because she was able to redirect her biological drives into creative ones. May Sinclair explained in *Feminism* (1912) how this redirection is possible:

> There is everything in that everlasting readiness to bring forth; everything in those profound and intarissable wells of instinct, in that stream of the Life-Force of which Woman is pre-eminently the reservoir. . . . For the Life-Force, like any other force when its channel is obstructed, will, of course, seek another; and it will tend to discharge itself along the line of least resistance. With your degenerate the line of least resistance may be the path of perdition. But with the normal, healthy human being, capable of control, may it not be transformed, transmuted, merged with certain increased energies of the body and the brain? In the artist, the enthusiast, the visionary (I will leave the saints out of this discussion), may it not be transformed and transmuted into still higher and subtler energies? [Pp. 30–31]

Concomitant with May Sinclair's portrayal of the determinism of sex is the problem of creativity. True to her biological image—the growth of the seed—is a concept of the genius who also conforms to an organic principle. In her closed world of necessity, genius is the only way one can overcome environmental determinism,[18] although even these individual overcomings of destiny may be illusory if genius itself is predetermined. It is a gift of the environment, a sudden flowering which derives from some confluence of the genes over which the individual has no control. However, when genius occurs in a combination with femininity in any of May Sinclair's novels, everything seems to go wrong. The various female characters in *The Creators* (1910),[19] for example, are all writers and must handle the impositions made upon their talents by romance and reproduction. The most talented of the women writers is nearly defeated by her maternity. In the years following her motherhood she skirts a nervous breakdown whenever she attempts a novel. One of the other characters has to lead a lonely, celibate life so that she can bring images to birth rather than children. Genius, "the divine thing," is seen here as something "subject to the law of the supersensible. To love anything more than this thing was to lose it. You had to come to it clean from all desire, naked of all possession." As a result, the demands of family life, of love, of responsibilities, go against it. In this novel one woman remarks that for genius, "virginity was the law, the indispensable condition" (pp. 116–17).

Ironically, in this novel May Sinclair allows a male character (who is also a writer) to express the connection between sex and creativity: "He denied perversely that genius was two-sexed, or that it was even essentially a virile thing. The fruitful genius was feminine, rather, humble and passive in its attitude to life. . . . All that it wanted, all that it could deal with was the germ, the undeveloped thing; the growing and shaping and bringing forth must be its own. The live thing, the thing that kicked, was never produced in any other way" (p. 15). This kind of genius, however, is "feminine" only in that it imitates the traditional concept of feminine receptivity: its passivity and its openness to physical reality. But the paradox is that this particular "femininity" may be more easily achieved by males.

18. The best example is Keith Rickman in *The Divine Fire* (New York: Henry Holt, 1905). See also the character of Tasker Jevons in *The Belfry* (New York: Macmillan, 1916).
19. May Sinclair, *The Creators: A Comedy* (New York: Century, 1910).

Obviously, this concept of the genius is not unique with May Sinclair. It derives from the basic nineteenth-century image of the genius which is most fully elaborated by Coleridge. However, May Sinclair uses the concept in relation to the feminine consciousness. Genius is the masculine form of creativity, corresponding with the feminine creation of life on the biological level. Other early twentieth-century writers, such as Shaw, were also concerned with this dichotomy, but May Sinclair used it very early to explain the problems of the female artist, and to relate them to the Freudian theory of sublimation, which she defined as "the diversion of the Life-Force, of the Will-to-live, from ways that serve the purposes and interests of species, into ways that serve the purposes and interests of individuals."[20] She distinguished between sublimation and repression: "Now the psychoanalysts tell you that wherever there is repression without sublimation there is neurosis or psychosis. It would be truer to say that wherever there is repression there is no sublimation, and wherever there is sublimation there is no repression. The Will-to-live has found another outlet."[21] Sublimation is achieved through choice. Nina Lempreier in *The Creators* never marries, loses the man she loves, but is then able to utilize her tremendous sexual energy in the creation of literature. This is sublimation. But with repression the result is illness, for then the energy which would have gone into sexuality and reproduction is turned not to the production of art but inward to one's own body.[22]

Mary Olivier sublimates rather than represses, but this distinction is not a simple one with her because her "feminine consciousness" is produced more by inhibitory factors than growth-encouraging ones. Her sense of self is obscure; she must search for it. She finds it difficult to separate her true being from the illusory one made up of connections with others—that self which is always in relation to something else; she sees herself as made up of

20. May Sinclair, *A Defence of Idealism: Some Questions and Conclusions* (New York: Macmillan, 1917), p. 7.
21. *Ibid.*
22. Instances of illness caused by repression may be found in Alice's hysteria in *The Three Sisters* and the wife's psychosomatic paralysis in *Life and Death of Harriet Frean*.

many "persons that were called Mary Olivier" (p. 94). She is her mother's daughter, her brother's sister, herself as a growing girl, and even something else. She calls that other self "her secret happiness" which "had nothing to do with any of these Mary Oliviers" (p. 94).

Her "secret happiness" is the key to her feminine consciousness, and later it is revealed as the only possible way for Mary to achieve "being." And it is at the beginning of Mary's search for identity as well as at its end. The more she thinks about her own "self," the more she wonders why she is told to forget about it, why she must suppress it:

> Your self? Your self? Why should you forget it? You had to remember. They would kill it if you let them.
>
> What had it done? What *was* it that they should hate it so? It had been happy and excited about *them*, wondering what they would be like. . . .
>
> Would it always have to stoop and cringe before people, hushing its own voice, hiding its own gesture? [P. 168]

These assertive desires always reflect that active part of her that her mother tried to suppress in order to make her "feminine." And it is this notion of femininity as passivity which seems to give her the most trouble. As Miriam Henderson also discovered, it is usually the basis for confusion and hostility. In order to do anything in the world, it is necessary to use active impulses. In order to be the conventional woman, the wife and helpmate of the nineteenth-century image of woman, it is necessary to be passive and quiescent. Mary builds a tower and knocks it over. She learns to play the piano and gives it up to please her parents. She has an affair with a man when she nears forty and leaves him in order to stay with her mother. She acts and then she retreats. All along she was capable of dynamic activity and strong sexual feelings. She had physical strength, in fact more of it than her brothers did. She lived with more imagination and verve. She should have been the one to travel and explore, to realize all her potentialities. Sexually, she was capable of fulfillment. The following passage hints at her ability to experience that fulfillment. It is not an overtly sexual passage (May Sinclair never does that—sexuality must be revealed through symbol and inference, never direct statement); instead, we have something that stands for it: "She let go the rail and drew herself up. A delicious thrill of danger went through her and out at her fingers. She flung herself into space and Mark caught her. His body felt hard and strong as it received her. They did it again and again. That was the 'faith-jump.' You knew that you would be killed if Mark didn't catch you, but you had faith that he would catch you; and he always did" (pp. 58–59). Mary is able to lose herself without fear. She can take daring chances. This is the kind of faith necessary for sexual orgasm—the ability to let oneself go and trust in the other, to let oneself die. This faith resembles religious faith, putting oneself in the hands of God. And eventually Mary is forced to choose that faith over the other. After a brief but ideal sexual relationship with Richard, a period where she is perfectly happy and fulfilled, she gives him up. Her long years of self-sacrifice and suppression have given her a life primarily of the mind. So much time had been devoted to fantasies, dreams, and unfulfilled wishes that when the real experience occurred, and she had her chance, she could not totally accept it. She needed to go on, by this time, and complete the direction her consciousness was taking. It would take her to the limits of egotism and beyond. It would take her out of herself at last.

The feminine consciousness as it emerges here—as in *Pilgrimage* —is primarily involved with the search for reality, reality as it can be perceived only by a woman. The major struggle with Mary, as it is revealed through her consciousness, is the struggle to become herself. And that "self," a feminine self, as Dorothy Richardson's Miriam also discovers, is found only in giving itself up. A profoundly mystical interpretation of life lies beneath the surface of this novel. Mary achieves "reality" only when she is able to lose herself. This Christian concept of salvation is directly related to the "femininity" which makes it possible. It comes easier to one who has been forced by environment and by determined sexual role to give up and to give in at every turn. A person whose life is spent fighting for the merest shreds of self-respect and independence of mind may more easily accept a relinquishment of self because that person knows that the self made up of experiences is so illusory. Mary Olivier understands her own process of self-making and, at the end, needs to get beyond the self she has created. She fought for it, won it in a lonely battle, and the battle forced her to accept a defeat that is also a victory: "When you lay still with your eyes shut and made the darkness come on, wave after wave, blotting out your body and the world, blotting out everything but your self and your will, that was a dying to live; a real dying, a real life" (p. 377).

But the new living must not be made up of the conflicts of the old, but in life that is without struggle, without ego. That old life and its conflicts were primarily related to sex: sexual role, sexual desire, and sexual conditioning. "Reality" must be a going beyond sex.

The feminine consciousness, then, in *Mary Olivier* becomes finally the ultimate passivity. It is the passivity Miriam Henderson achieved at moments in *Pilgrimage*, the passivity that allows one to be completely open to God and at one with all creation. Mary has glimpses of it throughout her life. It is what she calls her "secret happiness." It first occurs when she is a child, running alone past the houses in the neighborhood and out into the fields where she sees "a queer white light everywhere, like water thin and clear" (p. 48). She sees everything around her, the road, trees, cottages, taverns, all with the strange light on them. Then she sees everything as if "for the first time." Even when returning home, the sight of the house and everything within it is a suddenly new experience.

> The drawing-room at the back was full of the queer white light. Things stood out in it, sharp and suddenly strange, like the trees and houses in the light outside: the wine-red satin stripes in the grey damask curtains at the three windows; the rings of wine-red roses on the grey carpet; the tarnished pattern on the grey wallpaper; the furniture shining like dark wine; the fluted emerald green silk in the panel of the piano and the hanging bag of the

work-table; the small wine-red flowers on the pale green chintz; the green Chinese bowls in the rosewood cabinet; the blue and red parrot on the chair. [P. 49]

What is apparent about Mary's experience is that it presents her immediate perception of the things in themselves. She sees these various everyday objects as if for the first time, and in fact the phrase "saw . . . for the first time" is used three times in the whole description. This repetition emphasizes the spontaneous nature of her awareness. Her experience comes on by itself; it is not worked at, called for, in any way. It comes as a gift, a sudden seeing of the world as it is. In order to convey its essence, it is necessary for every detail to be described with precision, to show it in its individuality, in its very uniqueness, like "the rings of wine-red roses on the grey carpet." Yet the attempt is not completely successful because May Sinclair's use of similes and metaphors forces her to make comparisons, and ideally, in a mystical vision objects are comprehended because of their essential uniqueness, not because of their similarities. "Furniture shining like dark wine" is comparative. Yet perhaps May Sinclair is also trying to give the sense of correspondence, which is also a part of mystical awareness. Incidentally, the word "wine" may be symbolic, in fact symbolic in two directions. Traditionally it relates the experience to Christianity, and personally it refers to Mary's father, who was an alcoholic. However, any symbolism here appears incomplete and perhaps irrelevant.

The second part of the description of Mary's first mystical experience contains the human impact of that experience. When Mary sees her mother sitting in the room, she runs over to her and kisses her hands. And her mother only runs her hands over Mary's hair "with slight quick strokes that didn't stay, that didn't care" (p. 49). Her mother's lack of concern and obvious unawareness of Mary's state of mind affect Mary's rapture. Thus she leaves the room "very slowly, holding herself with care, lest she should jar her happiness and spill it" (p. 50). The passage ends with Mary back in her own room looking out the window: "Her happiness mixed itself up with the queer light and with the flat fields and the tall, bare trees. She turned from the window and saw the vases that Mamma had given her standing on the chimney-piece. . . . She threw herself on the bed and pressed her face into the pillow and cried 'Mamma! Mamma!' " (p. 50).

This long passage is one of the most important in the book. The *kind* of mystical experience that Mary undergoes here is characteristic of her personality. It is related to everyday things. It is a reaction against her sense of isolation and of feeling unloved by her mother, for whom she longs without limits. She has, then, a totally impersonal experience and it makes her happy. She does not try to *own* the objects she sees, nor does she blend herself in with them. But when she comes upon her mother and is forced to feel the separation between them, she experiences suddenly the fear of losing what has just happened. She becomes afraid that "she should jar her happiness and spill it." When the mystical awareness becomes self-conscious, when there arises the need to prolong it, to hold on to it, to possess it, then it must dissipate. For that kind of self-awareness is opposed to the nature of the experience. Therefore, after Mary leaves her mother she continues to feel what has happened, but it almost seems as if she forces it a little. When "her happiness mixed itself up with the queer light and with the flat fields and the tall, bare trees," the experience comes to an end. Then the sense of the things in themselves becomes mixed with her sense of her own self and her emotions. Then she must return to her normal state of mind, although it arrives with the helpless exasperation and longing of her cry for her mother.

Mary's "secret happiness" recurs sporadically, especially during adolescence, when it comes upon her very sharply and suddenly: "She could never tell when it was coming, nor what it would come from. It had something to do with the trees standing up in the golden white light" (p. 93). With adolescence comes Mary's intellectualization of the experience: "It had happened so often that she received it now with a shock of recognition; and when it was over she wanted it to happen again" (p. 93). She desires it to happen again, she tries to make it happen: "She would go back and back to the places where it had come, looking for it, thinking that any minute it might happen again" (pp. 93–94). But, of course, that is impossible. With adolescence also comes the inter-relationship between mystical perception and sexual desire: "Its thrill of reminiscence passed into the thrill of premonition, of something about to happen to her" (p. 125). The sensation of standing still in time, breathless, seeing into the essential nature of things, becomes bound up with the desire for completeness, for becoming one with them. The "thrill" then takes on sexual under-tones. Mary begins to discover her femininity and wants it ful-filled, and she associates the perfection of that fulfillment with what she previously experienced as her "secret happiness."[23]

By the time Mary reaches maturity, and after she has suffered disappointments which might have embittered her, she begins to place the mystical experience in its perspective as freedom in her life: "There was something in you that would go on, whatever happened. Whatever happened it would still be happy. Its hap-piness was not like the queer, sudden, uncertain ecstasy. She had never known *what* that was. . . . But that ecstasy and this happiness had one quality in common; they belonged to some part of you that was free. A you that had no hereditary destiny; that had got out of the net, or had never been caught in it" (pp. 311–12).

Contained within this sense of oneness and freedom is the way the self is released. It has "got out of the net." In fact, it is the only way in which the determinism of heredity and environment can be overcome. It is an idea that is not restricted in its applica-tion to women but is a possibility for everyone. What is "femi-nine," however, is the acceptance which always overcomes Mary, her need to sacrifice herself so continuously.

23. May Sinclair explained the connection between the intense experience of communion with nature and physiological drives in *Feminism* (1912): "Whoever has known and can remember certain moments of heightened vision and sensation, when things seen—common things—trees in a field—a stretch of sky—became transfigured and took on I know not what divine radiance and beauty, whoever has known the exaltation, the exquisite and unspeakable joy, the sheer ecstasy and the ultimate peace that accompany such vision, . . . will remain unmoved while the physiologist points out that these moments are most intimately associated with adolescence and the dawn of womanhood; that they are incident to falling in love; that they are part of the pageant of sexual passion, the psychological side of the great decorative illusion by which the Life-Force lures us to its end" (p. 31).

Mary Olivier ends with Mary trying to make the connection between determinism and freedom clear in this very special sense. Her final realization involves, quite simply, accepting the will of God:

> If you were part of God your will was God's will at the moment when you really willed. There was always a point when you knew it: the flash point of freedom. You couldn't mistake your flash when it came. You couldn't doubt away that certainty of freedom any more than you could doubt away the certainty of necessity and determination. From the outside they were part of the show of existence, the illusion of separation from God. From the inside they were God's will, the way things were willed. Free-will was the reality underneath the illusion of necessity. The flash point of freedom was your consciousness of God. [Pp. 376–77]

Three

Virginia Woolf

Turning to Virginia Woolf's novels after Dorothy Richardson's relentless interior realism and May Sinclair's careful, craftsmanlike portraits has the effect of a dam bursting. The stream now flows recklessly, carrying with it a profusion of wild and beautiful imagery. Before long, the reader becomes aware that descriptions of consciousness are no longer to be considered primarily as the method for a more accurate analysis of character, but that consciousness in her novels is a means to get at the essence of life itself. The great mystery of human personality and its connections with ultimate reality, rather than the psychic development of one individual such as one finds in Richardson and Sinclair, become the focus. Virginia Woolf (1882–1941) seems to infer a mysticism which may be approached mainly through metaphor (that "luminous halo" and "semi-transparent envelope" she refers to in her much-quoted essay),[1] and which leads to a treatment of consciousness in which imagery is a predominant device. This results from her need to express what is inexpressible and paradoxical. She has no interest in a scientific rendering of the contents of the mind; the "stream of consciousness" is to be

1. Virginia Woolf, "Modern Fiction," in *The Common Reader, First Series* (New York: Harvest Books, 1954), p. 154.

ordered into an artistic pattern. For Virginia Woolf the concern
is with art and its connections with spiritual experience. Like
Dorothy Richardson and May Sinclair, she explores the feminine
consciousness with the ultimate aim of reaching enlightenment,
but unlike them, she emphasizes its necessary connection with
artistic creation. While Miriam Henderson and Mary Olivier *tell*
us about their mystical awareness, Virginia Woolf's characters
allow us to *experience* "reality" through our own spontaneous
identification with what is revealed.[2]

Consequently, the complete realization of feminine consciousness is not the final goal for Virginia Woolf as it was for the others.
Feminine consciousness and mystical awareness became one entity for their characters. With Virginia Woolf, feminine consciousness is explored as part of reality, but ultimate reality can
only be perceived by going beyond it. Only in the highest form
of creativity, in which there is a moment of vision caught and
eternalized in *form,* is universal consciousness achieved. And there
distinctions between sexes must disappear. Only the "androgynous" is capable of this fullness of vision. And it is this understanding of the bisexual quality of consciousness which sets
Virginia Woolf apart from Dorothy Richardson and May Sinclair, who were aware of this condition but did not work out
theories to incorporate it. Miriam Henderson, for example, tries
to overcome masculine traits in her consciousness, Mary Olivier,
to suppress them. But Virginia Woolf expands the notion of
androgyny and uses it as a symbol of unity.

It is within this context that I would like to consider feminine
consciousness in Virginia Woolf's characters. The masculine as-

2. My concern here is not with Virginia Woolf as a person; I focus upon the
consciousnesses of her female characters. For biographical information, the best
source is Quentin Bell's *Virginia Woolf: A Biography* (New York: Harcourt Brace
Jovanovich, 1972). A most helpful and insightful account of Virginia Woolf's
actual methods of organizing consciousness—based in part on materials gathered
from the Virginia Woolf manuscripts in the Berg Collection—is Harvena Richter's
Virginia Woolf: The Inward Voyage (Princeton, N.J.: Princeton University Press,
1970). For a study of the relationship between Virginia Woolf's ideas about
feminism and her novels, see Herbert Marder, *Feminism and Art: A Study of Virginia Woolf* (Chicago: University of Chicago Press, 1968).

pects of the consciousness of women and the dual nature of sexual identity will be part of this chapter's concerns. The specific feminism of Dorothy Richardson—which asserts the absolute superiority of feminine modes of thought—is not really possible within an androgynous model, even though Virginia Woolf's characters may express it at times.[3]

Although May Sinclair and Dorothy Richardson preceded Virginia Woolf in their use of the stream of consciousness as content for their novels, it is not at all certain that she was influenced by them. In fact, there is very little evidence to show that she ever read May Sinclair at all. She never reviewed any of her novels, nor did she comment on them in her diaries.[4] But with Dorothy Richardson, the possibility of influence is much greater. Virginia Woolf wrote two reviews of Dorothy Richardson's fiction before publishing *Mrs. Dalloway*. However, Leonard Woolf remarks in his autobiography that Virginia wrote "The Mark on the Wall," in which she used an interior approach, before reading Dorothy Richardson's *The Tunnel*.[5] What is most probable is that Virginia Woolf recognized a similar attitude when she referred to "the method" which "should make us feel ourselves seated at the centre of another mind." But she also insisted that "we should

3. Marder provides a helpful summary of the general meaning of the androgynous for Virginia Woolf: "Virginia Woolf saw the universe as the scene of an eternal conflict between opposites, corresponding, roughly speaking, to masculine and feminine principles. Her main concern was to find ways of reconciling the warring opposites. As a practical feminist she sought equality between the sexes, a dynamic balance between the two halves of mankind which would lead to social regeneration. As artist and mystic she sought inner harmony, the ideal state of androgyny, which would lead to the renewal of the individual. Psychic freedom must wait on political freedom, however, for how could women achieve harmony until they were free of a sense of grievance? One might say that, for Virginia Woolf, feminism and mysticism converged in the doctrine of androgyny" (p. 125).

4. The only place I have discovered May Sinclair's name in any of Virginia Woolf's published writings is in her response to a letter from Lytton Strachey. He wrote on Feb. 10, 1922: "May Sinclair's book, 'The Life and Death of Harriet[t] Frean' has some merit, though nasty. Have you seen it?" She answered on Feb. 11, 1922: "And you read Miss Sinclair! So shall I perhaps. But I'd rather read Lytton Strachey." These quotations are from Virginia Woolf's and Lytton Strachey's *Letters*, ed. Leonard Woolf and James Strachey (London: Hogarth Press, 1956), pp. 99–100.

5. Leonard Woolf, *Downhill All the Way: An Autobiography of the Years 1919–1939* (London: Hogarth Press, 1968), p. 59.

perceive in the helter-skelter of flying fragments some unity, significance, or design."[6]

Virginia Woolf's demand for "design" immediately sets her apart from Dorothy Richardson and indicates the direction she was to take, which would lead her far beyond interior realism. In her review of *Revolving Lights* in 1923 her appreciation of Dorothy Richardson's procedures is illustrated even more acutely:

> There is no one word, such as romance or realism, to cover, even roughly, the works of Miss Dorothy Richardson. Their chief characteristic, if an intermittent student be qualified to speak, is one for which we still seek a name. She has invented, or, if she has not invented, developed and applied to her own uses, a sentence which we might call the psychological sentence of the feminine gender. It is of a more elastic fibre than the old, capable of stretching to the extreme, of suspending the frailest particles, of enveloping the vaguest shapes. Other writers of the opposite sex have used sentences of this description and stretched them to the extreme. But there is a difference. Miss Richardson has fashioned her sentence consciously, in order that it may descend to the depths and investigate the crannies of Miriam Henderson's consciousness. It is a woman's sentence, but only in the sense that it is used to describe a woman's mind by a writer who is neither proud nor afraid of anything that she may discover in the psychology of her sex. . . . Her discoveries are concerned with states of being and not with states of doing. Miriam is aware of "life itself"; of the atmosphere of the table rather than of the table; of the silence rather than of the sound. Therefore she adds an element to her perception of things which has not been noticed before, or, if noticed, has been guiltily suppressed. A man might fall dead at her feet (it is not likely), and Miriam might feel that a violet coloured ray of light was an important element in her consciousness of the tragedy. If she felt it, she would say it.[7]

Not only does the preceding passage indicate Virginia Woolf's sympathy with Dorothy Richardson, but it also summarizes her own direction in literature. One can discover in it four areas of

6. Virginia Woolf, review of *The Tunnel* in *Contemporary Writers* (New York: Harcourt, Brace, 1966), p. 121.

7. Virginia Woolf, review of *Revolving Lights* in *Contemporary Writers*, pp. 124–25.

concern which she will develop in her own writing. The beginning
sentence refers to the rejection of traditional forms which Virginia Woolf felt was necessary in order to approach "life itself."
The second area is the investigation of the feminine mind; this
she was shortly to bring to a high order of perfection in *Mrs.
Dalloway*. Next is her understanding of Dorothy Richardson's
interest in "states of being and not with states of doing." This she
prefers to the descriptions of external behavior and surfaces which
she objects to in Bennett, Wells, and Galsworthy.[8] Last, and
most important in terms of the focus of this chapter, is her description of Dorothy Richardson's "psychological sentence of the
feminine gender."

For Virginia Woolf had commented in 1929 on the difficulties
faced by the woman writer in having to use a sentence structure
invented by men:

> But it is still true that before a woman can write exactly as she
> wishes to write, she has many difficulties to face. To begin with,
> there is the technical difficulty—so simple, apparently; in reality,
> so baffling—that the very form of the sentence does not fit her.
> It is a sentence made by men; it is too loose, too heavy, too
> pompous for a woman's use. Yet in a novel, which covers so wide
> a stretch of ground, an ordinary and usual type of sentence has
> to be found to carry the reader on easily and naturally from one
> end of the book to the other. And this a woman must make for
> herself, altering and adapting the current sentence until she writes
> one that takes the natural shape of her thought without crushing
> or distorting it.[9]

Once Virginia Woolf, like Dorothy Richardson, centered her
attention on the inner life, it became increasingly important for
her to communicate patterns of thinking in sentences that were
capable of handling the complexity of the feminine consciousness. In an article exploring the structure of sentences in stream-
of-consciousness fiction, Liisa Dahl discovers that Virginia Woolf

---

8. Virginia Woolf, "Mr. Bennett and Mrs. Brown," in *The Captain's Death
Bed and Other Essays* (New York: Harcourt, Brace, 1950), pp. 94–119.

9. Virginia Woolf, "Women and Fiction," in *Collected Essays*, II (London:
Hogarth Press, 1966), 145.

generally uses what she calls the "rounded impressionistic sentence."[10] This is a sentence in which the chain of separate modifiers is bound up with some part that connects the sentence to its starting point. Sentences of this type are connected very loosely, and are ideal for communicating emotionally charged thought sequences in which no one idea is subordinate to any other.[11]

In the following passage from *Mrs. Dalloway*,[12] one can discover the sentence in its typical form and also Mrs. Dalloway's method of ordering physical objects in her consciousness:

There were flowers: delphiniums, sweet peas, bunches of lilac; and carnations, masses of carnations. There were roses; there were irises. Ah yes—so she breathed in the earthy garden sweet smell as she stood talking to Miss Pym who owed her help, and thought her kind, for kind she had been years ago; very kind, but she looked older, this year, turning her head from side to side among the irises and roses and nodding tufts of lilac with her eyes half closed, snuffing in, after the street uproar, the delicious scent, the exquisite coolness. And then, opening her eyes, how fresh like frilled linen clean from a laundry laid in wicker trays the roses looked; and dark and prim the red carnations, holding their heads up; and all the sweet peas spreading in their bowls, tinged violet, snow white, pale—as if it were the evening and girls in muslin frocks came out to pick sweet peas and roses after the superb summer's day, with its almost blue-black sky, its delphiniums, its carnations its arum liles was over; and it was the moment between six and seven when every flower—roses, carnations, irises, lilac—glows; white, violet, red, deep orange; every flower seems to

10. Liisa Dahl, "The Attributive Sentence Structure in the Stream-of-Consciousness-Technique. With Special Reference to the Interior Monologue Used by Virginia Woolf, James Joyce, and Eugene O'Neill," *Neuphilologische Mitteilungen*, 68 (1967), 443.

11. Even an early critic of Virginia Woolf, Ruth Gruber, was attuned to the connection between Clarissa's personality and the sentence structure Virginia Woolf used to explore it: "She is a compound writer rather than a complex one; her thoughts are ordered in *ands* and *buts*. Her sentences are clever windings and turnings of gushing irrelevancies. . . . The thoughts run on like a gossipy woman; the long full sentence is less a structural feat than a psychologic one, giving the hurrying, bustling tokens of the hurrying, bustling observations and ideas. It is such writing which makes "Mrs. Dalloway" the unquestionable product of a woman" (*Virginia Woolf: A Study* (Leipzig: Tauchnitz, 1935), p. 46).

12. Virginia Woolf, *Mrs. Dalloway* (New York: Harcourt, Brace, 1925).

burn by itself, softly, purely in the misty beds; and how she loved the grey-white moths spinning in and out, over the cherry pie, over the evening primroses! [Pp. 17–18]

The sentence beginning "Ah yes—so she breathed in the earthy garden sweet smell . . ." is quite illustrative. Within it one finds Clarissa's exclamation "Ah yes" followed by the immediate sensory perception of the smell from the flowers, then a reflection upon the visual perception of Miss Pym, and then a consideration of her own appearance and how it had changed, all the while being aware of the smell of that immediate moment (and separating that moment from the one which preceded it: "after the street uproar"). The kind of movement from self to the object of perception, to self again, to past and immediate past and present, the movement from perception to reflection and back again is characteristic of these sentences which illustrate the movements of the mind.

As one continues reading the passage, one also becomes aware of the deliberately "feminine" associations set up in the imagery. "Fresh like frilled linen clean from a laundry" connects with the freshness of muslin frocks. They seem to be associated with her memories of girlhood, memories of the summer nights which she will remember with greater detail in the novel when she thinks about Sally Seton and Peter Walsh.

Clarissa's awareness of the physical world and its objects is usually clear and precise. The objects are delineated sharply, without blurring, because each perception is involved in a moment of absolute stillness:

> The hall of the house was cool as a vault. Mrs. Dalloway raised her hand to her eyes, and, as the maid shut the door to, and she heard the swish of Lucy's skirts, she felt like a nun who has left the world and feels fold round her the familiar veils and the response to old devotions. The cook whistled in the kitchen. She heard the click of the typewriter. It was her life, and, bending her head over the hall table, she bowed beneath the influence, felt blessed and purified, saying to herself, as she took the pad with the telephone message on it, how moments like this are buds on

the tree of life, flowers of darkness they are, she thought (as if some lovely rose had blossomed for her eyes only); not for a moment did she believe in God; but all the more, she thought, taking up the pad, must one repay in daily life to servants, yet, to dogs and canaries, above all to Richard her husband, who was the foundation of it—of the gay sounds, of the green lights, of the cook even whistling, for Mrs. Walker was Irish and whistled all day long—one must pay back from this secret deposit of exquisite moments, she thought, lifting the pad, while Lucy stood by her, trying to explain how [Pp. 42–43]

Here the images are especially concrete: "the swish of Lucy's skirts," "the click of the typewriter." She is able to communicate the sounds which accompany the overwhelming sense of silence. She gives out a sense of being protected, cloistered from the world. The security of the "house" and her own withdrawal from connections with others, at moments like this where she observes her own solitude, are important manifestations of the kind of feminine consciousness Virginia Woolf was developing for her character. And as in the earlier passage the sensory perceptions of flowers provided the starting point for reflection, here other specific objects provide the starting point which will lead her to reflect upon flowers. Flowers in both cases are associated with precious moments, and here, as well as in other instances, flower imagery relates to a feminine mental fertility.

II   Another conventionally feminine reaction in the last-quoted passage from *Mrs. Dalloway* is Clarissa's consideration of self-sacrifice. I will talk about this later in another context, but right here Clarissa thinks she must "repay in daily life" for "this secret deposit of exquisite moments." Never does she consider these special moments as gratuitous. In *To the Lighthouse* Mrs. Ramsay has this same sense of self-sacrifice, and the knowledge that at any moment the beautiful might be snuffed out.[13]

It is even possible to compare Clarissa's concrete apprehension

13. Mrs. Ramsay feels "life terrible, hostile, and quick to pounce on you if you gave it a chance" (*To the Lighthouse* (New York: Harcourt, Brace, 1927), p. 92).

of the world about her with that of Mary Olivier. The following passage is rather reminiscent of Mary's description of her "secret happiness":

> Laying her brooch on the table, she had a sudden spasm, as if, while she mused, the icy claws had had the chance to fix in her. She was not old yet. She had just broken into her fifty-second year. Months and months of it were still untouched. June, July, August! Each still remained almost whole, and, as if to catch the falling drop, Clarissa (crossing to the dressing-table) plunged into the very heart of the moment, transfixed it, there—the moment of this June morning on which was the pressure of all the other mornings, seeing the glass, the dressing-table, and all the bottles afresh, collecting the whole of her at one point (as she looked into the glass), seeing the delicate pink face of the woman who was that very night to give a party; of Clarissa Dalloway; of herself. [P. 54]

Clarissa *sees* the objects before her with superclarity. But she does not go on to feel the tremendous happiness that Mary Olivier experienced during her moment of insight, although something similar to that happiness is evident in the previous passage. Moreover, Clarissa's consciousness incorporates images more readily than Miriam's or Mary's. Correspondences between specific physical objects and forces in nature occur repeatedly. These give the impression of the unity of all things, of which an individual consciousness is but a small part. Whereas the moments of correspondence occur only at high points in the novels of the other two women, they are almost continually evident in the consciousnesses of Virginia Woolf's characters:

> Quiet descended on her, calm, content, as her needle, drawing the silk smoothly to its gentle pause, collected the green folds together and attached them, very lightly, to the belt. So on a summer's day waves collect, overbalance, and fall; collect and fall; and the whole world seems to be saying "that is all" more and more ponderously, until even the heart in the body which lies in the sun on the beach says too, That is all. . . . Fear no more, says the heart, committing its burden to some sea, which sighs

collectively for all sorrows, and renews, begins, collects, lets fall. And the body alone listens to the passing bee; the wave breaking; the dog barking, far away barking and barking. [Pp. 58–59]

Part of the suggestion of universality in this passage may be explained by considering the role of the narrator. There are subtle shifts away from Clarissa's consciousness to the more general voice of an omniscient narrator. In some sections of Virginia Woolf's writing the boundaries between consciousnesses are so loose and shifting that one cannot be certain where one consciousness ends and another begins.[14] But here it seems that the explanation of the narrator actually takes up the body of the passage. It is more a comment upon the mood and atmosphere of Clarissa's thought than a direct revelation of it.

Virginia Woolf not only attempts to achieve unity through the use of correspondences, but she also suggests that consciousness itself is not a completely isolated phenomenon in which each human being is locked into its own limited consciousness. Since consciousness is not necessarily self-contained, images and reflections of the other characters may be as important as self-reflections. Mrs. Dalloway does not live for us only through her own consciousness of herself, as do Miriam Henderson and Mary Olivier. In fact, Virginia Woolf goes even further and implies the basic diffuseness of consciousness itself. There is much of what Harvena Richter calls "the impression of a mass mind individualized"[15] in Virginia Woolf's novels. The most obvious example is her use of Septimus Smith as a "double" for Clarissa.[16]

14. A most helpful elaboration of Virginia Woolf's handling of different narrators and "voices" is Mitchell A. Leaska's *Virginia Woolf's Lighthouse: A Study in Critical Method* (New York: Columbia University Press, 1970).

15. Richter, p. 53.

16. Dr. Jean Love remarks that "the construction of *Mrs. Dalloway* . . . establishes that consciousness is truly diffuse. Rather than being composed of individual emanations, it is a property of the whole, of the universe. This is the basis of Clarissa Dalloway's oneness with Septimus Smith whom she never meets in the flesh and with Peter Walsh whom she had almost married. The seamless quality of consciousness precludes true individuality and therefore precludes an external amalgamation of consciousness from individual sources" (Jean O. Love, *Worlds in Consciousness: Mythopoetic Thought in the Novels of Virginia Woolf* (Berkeley and Los Angeles: University of California Press, 1970), p. 42). Alex Page

Clarissa, in particular, seems to yearn toward whatever might complete herself. Thus she is drawn toward people who represent unity. Older now, and weak, she admires physical activity in others; their motion and energy, similar to what she sees reflected in nature, are what she longs for herself: "waves of that divine vitality which Clarissa loved. To dance, to ride, she had adored all that" (p. 9). She is similar in this respect to Jinny in *The Waves* (1931): "I move, I dance; I never cease to move and to dance."[17] So Clarissa loves youth because it has this ability to be active: "For the young people could not talk; and why should they? Shout, embrace, swing, be up at dawn; carry sugar to ponies; kiss and caress the snouts of adorable chows; and then all tingling and streaming, plunge and swim" (p. 270).

Clarissa is interested in people's reactions to her physical presence; part of her feminine consciousness is her own physical self-image: "How much she wanted it—that people should look pleased as she came in" (p. 13).[18] However, in moments of unhappiness she belittles her own body and insists upon its unimportance, downgrading her femininity, which she feels to be the cause of her misery. She compares herself with Lady Bexborough and remarks upon her own "narrow pea-stick figure" and "ridiculous little face, beaked like a bird's": "But often now this body she wore . . . this body, with all its capacities, seemed nothing—nothing at all. She had the oddest sense of being herself invisible; unseen; unknown; there being no more marrying, no more having of children now; but only this astonishing and rather solemn progress with the rest of them, up Bond Street, this being Mrs. Dalloway; not even Clarissa any more; this being Mrs. Richard Dalloway" (p. 14). Her insignificance is made greater at the end

---

describes Clarissa and Septimus as a double personality, with Clarissa "as the highly conscious ego of a double personality" and Septimus as the id! ("A Dangerous Day: Mrs. Dalloway Discovers Her Double," *Modern Fiction Studies*, 7 (Summer, 1961), 115–24.)

17. Virginia Woolf, *The Waves* (New York: Harcourt, Brace, 1931), p. 42.

18. Mrs. Ramsay was also aware of her physical beauty and its effect upon others: "And after all—after all (here insensibly she drew herself together, physically, the sense of her own beauty becoming, as it did so seldom, present to her)—after all, she had not generally any difficulty in making people like her" (*To the Lighthouse*, p. 64).

of the passage in her subtle resentment against the merging of a
wife's identity with her husband's: not Clarissa anymore but "Mrs.
Richard."

Another element in Mrs. Dalloway's consciousness of herself
is her ability to feel physical sensations related to emotional reactions. For example, when disturbed by her own hostility against
Miss Kilman, she reflects on "this hatred, which, especially since
her illness, had power to make her feel scraped, hurt in her spine;
gave her physical pain" (p. 17). Again, when she hears of Septimus's death, she reflects that "always her body went through it
first, when she was told, suddenly, of an accident; her dress flamed,
her body burnt" (p. 280).

Clarissa loses the sense of her body, however, when she is totally
at one with what is happening, such as when at the height of her
success at the party she becomes tired of the effort to pull everything together:

> She was not enjoying it. It was too much like being—just anybody,
> standing there; anybody could do it; yet this anybody she did a
> little admire, couldn't help feeling that she had, anyhow, made
> this happen, that it marked a stage, this post that she felt herself
> to have become, for oddly enough she had quite forgotten what
> she looked like, but felt herself a stake driven in at the top of her
> stairs. Every time she gave a party she had this feeling of being
> something not herself, and that every one was unreal in one way;
> much more real in another. [P. 259]

Clarissa's loss of the sense of her body in moments of high excitement or exhaustion is but another aspect of that diffusion of self
I mentioned earlier. Clarissa often has trouble holding on to her
identity. For instance, when she looks at herself in a mirror—
noticing her face and having a point of reference—she still has
trouble holding on to it:

> How many million times she had seen her face, and always
> with the same imperceptible contradiction! She pursed her lips
> when she looked in the glass. It was to give her face point. That
> was her self—pointed; dartlike; definite. That was her self when
> some effort, some call on her to be her self, drew the parts to-

gether, she alone knew how different, how incompatible and composed so for the world only into one centre, one diamond, one woman who sat in her drawing-room and made a meeting-point, a radiancy no doubt in some dull lives. . . . [P. 55]

Clarissa not only realizes that she must make an effort to pull the parts of herself together (Rhoda, in *The Waves*, tries but is never able to achieve a sense of her own self, even momentarily; she is always diffused), but she recognizes this same diffuseness in the world around her. This makes her slow to judge. She does not like men's rigid black/white distinctions; she does not like to label or pin down: "She would not say of anyone in the world now that they were this or were that. She felt very young; at the same time unspeakably aged. She sliced like a knife through everything; at the same time was outside, looking on" (p. 11). Clarissa's opposition to categorizing is slightly different from Miriam Henderson's, however. With respect to the opposition between reason and intuition which seems to be implied, Virginia Woolf stresses the difficulties of consciousness itself as a reason for preferring spontaneous understanding to rigid categorizing dealing only with surface entities. Men like Bradshaw make an arbitrary consolidation of the fragments of consciousness into a whole which must conform to a preconceived pattern. But a woman like Clarissa, who recognizes the diffuseness, refuses to judge so severely. She has a fluidity that Bradshaw lacks. Miriam Henderson has a much stronger sense of self, an egotism that centers experience for herself on herself; she does not feel as if she is coming apart. Virginia Woolf recognizes a greater tenuousness of personality. As another contrast, with May Sinclair personality is determined by heredity and environment and thus is firm and clear. Characters are types determined by their upbringing. Even mental illness is portrayed in terms of excessive intensity of symptoms true to a character's personality: alcoholism, nymphomania, etc. Never is it shown as the disintegration of ego. Septimus Smith, Rhoda, and even Clarissa herself vibrate along with that "incessant shower of innumerable atoms" and are basically as fragmented as the reality outside themselves.

Rhoda in *The Waves* has so little power over the impressions impinging on her senses and emanating from her unconscious that she has to fight for a sense of reality. She feels "I am broken into separate pieces; I am no longer one" (p. 106). She has no grasp of her own oneness, and reveals it in her "hopeless desire to be Susan, to be Jinny" (p. 27), to become the other. She carries envy and self-abnegation to their furthest limits. Yet instead of sublimating her feelings in idolization, she recognizes them overtly and *knows* she wants to *be* the other. Her need to pull herself together is so great that she often tries to reach out to inanimate things to gain control: "I will assure myself, touching the rail of something hard. Now I cannot sink; cannot altogether fall through the thin sheet now" (p. 27).[19] There almost seems to be a suggestion that her very molecules can pass through walls and physical barriers (she is so in touch with her own atomistic makeup, both physically and mentally). She is even unable to accept the common notion of cause and effect, of the connection between one thing and another. Thus time itself is disconnected. "One moment does not lead to another. The door opens and the tiger leaps. . . . I cannot make one moment merge in the next. To me they are all violent, all separate" (p. 130).

Of course Clarissa is not as extreme. Her ability to be in tune with the diffuseness of consciousness—which is the cause of her refusal to label and to thereby make things rigid and permanent —is a reflection of her acceptance of transcience. She can delight in the moment, in the pure joy of one moment and the next and the next, instead of objectifying them and making them heavy. Thus she often contrasts this sense of life which she feels with the abstractions made by men about living. She compares herself with Peter Walsh and realizes their difference: "But Peter—however beautiful the day might be, and the trees and the grass, and the little girl in pink—Peter never saw a thing of all that. He would

19. The persona in Virginia Woolf's "The Mark on the Wall" expresses wonder that it is possible to maintain any sense of solidity in life: "The wonder is that I've any clothes on my back, that I sit surrounded by solid furniture at this moment" (in *A Haunted House and Other Short Stories* (New York: Harcourt, Brace & World, 1944), p. 38).

put on his spectacles, if she told him to; he would look. It was the state of the world that interested him; Wagner, Pope's poetry, people's characters eternally, and the defects of her own soul" (p. 9). "People's characters eternally": an apt phrase and in permanent opposition to the specific visions Clarissa has of the ceaseless changes of life. When she contrasts her own lack of education with Peter's knowledge, "she knew nothing; no language, no history; she scarcely read a book now, except memoirs in bed"; she defends her ignorance by saying that "to her it was absolutely absorbing; all this; the cabs passing; and she would not say of Peter, she would not say of herself, I am this, I am that." Thus she opposes book knowledge to the truth of life. The very next line gives the answer: "Her only gift was knowing people almost by instinct, she thought, walking on" (p. 11).

Like Miriam Henderson, Clarissa stresses her own intuitive grasp of life over the rational, not organizing life in categories, emphasizing essences of things. Because she is so close to the idea of death, she is immediately aware of life's ephemeral nature yet able to experience the present in its completeness. "She remembered once throwing a shilling into the Serpentine. But every one remembered; what she loved was this, here, now, in front of her; the fat lady in the cab" (p. 12). The specific, the even ugly present, is what she holds on to. Remembering—friends and events— is different from present loving. But in spite of her passion for the moment, she hopes for more: that the possibility of diffused consciousness might ease the pain of finality:

> Did it matter then, she asked herself . . . did it matter that she must inevitably cease completely; all this must go on without her; did she resent it; or did it not become consoling to believe that death ended absolutely? but that somehow in the streets of London, on the ebb and flow of things, here, there, she survived, Peter survived, lived in each other, she being part, she was positive, of the trees at home; of the house there, ugly, rambling all to bits and pieces as it was; part of people she had never met; being laid out like a mist between the people she knew best, who lifted her on their branches as she had seen the trees lift the mist, but it spread ever so far, her life, herself. [P. 12]

III   Clarissa's desire for self-unity, for a sense of her self, as
well as a means of making that self permanent, is reflected
in the preceding passages. And these are all related to the meta-
physical problems which are basic in this novel. But her sexual
identification—the pulling herself together as a woman—is also an
issue in her consciousness. And the problem of femininity is closely
linked with the problem of self in general. J. B. Batchelor identifies Clarissa Dalloway with those women in Virginia Woolf's
novels who attempt to define themselves as women by rejecting
the male and retreating into an interior world, pure and isolated,[20]
and surely one can discover elements of hostility in Clarissa's relations with men—at least in her reflections upon them. Her mental argument with Peter Walsh is illustrative. She argues against
his accusations years after they were said. She hates anyone to
force her, to compel her, to think one way or another. She dislikes
Sir William Bradshaw because he is "capable of some indescrib-
able outrage—forcing your soul." (This is reminiscent of Miriam
Henderson's rejection of Hypo Wilson because he, too, tried to
force her soul.)

Clarissa remembers her arguments with Peter and uses them
to justify her decision not to marry him. Peter tried to force intimacy. "But with Peter everything had to be shared; everything
gone into," while she believed that "in marriage a little license, a
little independence there must be between people living together
day in day out in the same house; which Richard gave her, and
she him" (p. 10). Conversely, these arguments point up how
much Peter has meant to her: "Yet, after all, how much she owed
to him later. Always when she thought of him she thought of their
quarrels for some reason—because she wanted his good opinion so
much, perhaps. She owed him words: 'sentimental,' 'civilized';
they started up every day of her life as if he guarded her" (pp. 53–
54). Peter labels while she refrains from labeling, but nonetheless
he provides that masculine contrast, that opposing view to her
own.

Clarissa's sexual consciousness is ambivalent in a way quite

20. J. B. Batchelor, "Feminism in Virginia Woolf," *English* (London), 17
(Spring, 1968), 6.

similar to Miriam Henderson's. This is especially interesting in light of the tremendous differences between the two characters. Miriam is obsessed with the idea of freedom; she is independent. Clarissa is a married woman, safe in a dependent relationship, the same kind of relationship, in fact, that Miriam imagines for herself with Densley. Miriam foresees a central loneliness in life with a man who could worship her femininity and respect her role as a woman but who would be unable to share in her inner life. She is in conflict between a remote and kind man—a man who would respect her privacy and not attempt to mold her mind—and the others, represented by Michael and especially by Hypo Wilson, who would argue and pull at her, forcing her to lose any sense of her identity by making her defensive. Miriam escapes from the conflict altogether by choosing isolation. Clarissa Dalloway once had the same choice. There was Richard Dalloway, who would allow for "a dignity in people; a solitude; even between husband and wife a gulf; and that one must respect . . . for one would not part with it oneself, or take it, against his will, from one's husband, without losing one's independence, one's self-respect—something, after all, priceless" (p. 181). And there was Peter Walsh, who needed to "share" everything. Clarissa made the choice; she did not escape from it by choosing neither. She chose Richard, and her choice allowed her internal freedom—but also that essential loneliness.

Clarissa's great need to maintain her identity and prevent its dissolution into innumerable fragments figures in her physical coldness. She has an image of herself as nunlike in her attic room (this image connects with the earlier quoted passage where she imagines her house as a vault):

> So the room was an attic; the bed narrow; and lying there reading, for she slept badly, she could not dispel a virginity preserved through childbirth which clung to her like a sheet. Lovely in girlhood, suddenly there came a moment—for example on the river beneath the woods at Clieveden—when, through some contraction of this cold spirit, she had failed him. And then at Constantinople, and again and again. She could see what she lacked. It was not beauty; it was not mind. It was something central

which permeated; something warm which broke up surfaces and
rippled the cold contact of man and woman, or of women together. [P. 46]

The "something central" to which she refers is the ability to
lose hold of the ego, and not to fear this letting go, to allow for a
spontaneous communion of bodies and minds. Rhoda in *The
Waves* shares this condition of physical coldness. But Rhoda's
frigidity is at the extreme. She is afraid of sex. She says, "I feared
embraces" (p. 205). One might even say that she hated sex as
well. She speaks of the trees on the avenue being "obscene with
lovers" (p. 216). Fear and dislike of sexuality grow out of her
primary fear of physicality itself. She is horrified to be close to
other people: "I should stand in a queue; and smell sweat, and
scent as horrible as sweat; and be hung with other people like a
joint of meat among other joints of meat" (pp. 161–62).

Clarissa's coldness hardly goes this far. She can at least *imagine*
how she should be and can experience physical passion—even
though it is with women rather than men:

> For *that* [the element lacking for her with Richard] she could
> dimly perceive. She resented it, had a scruple picked up Heaven
> knows where, or, as she felt, sent by Nature (who is invariably
> wise); yet she could not resist sometimes yielding to the charm
> of a woman, not a girl . . . she did undoubtedly then feel what
> men felt. Only for a moment; but it was enough. It was a sudden
> revelation, a tinge like a blush which one tried to check and then,
> as it spread, one yielded to its expansion, and rushed to the far-
> thest verge and there quivered and felt the world come closer,
> swollen with some astonishing significance, some pressure of rap-
> ture, which split its thin skin and gushed and poured with an ex-
> traordinary alleviation over the cracks and sores! Then, for that
> moment, she had seen an illumination; a match burning in a
> crocus; an inner meaning almost expressed. But the close with-
> drew; the hard softened. It was over—the moment. [Pp. 46–47]

Bisexuality is much more a conscious element in Clarissa's mind
than it was in Miriam's. Of course, the difference in awareness
(explicated by labeling it for what it is, "this falling in love with
women" (p. 48)) may be partly explained by remarking that

Clarissa's understanding of the feeling comes years after the event. Her love for Sally is only part of her consciousness, as memory. With Miriam, the reader is given a present view of her feelings. But like Miriam, Clarissa seems able to experience a totally unself-conscious passion only with another woman. Clarissa experiences a reversal of roles when she imaginatively assumes the male role in her love for Sally Seton. Sally, by the way, is remarkably similar to Amabel in *Pilgrimage*. She is physically appealing—wild, high-spirited, daring—a perfect object of envy for the cold, reflective woman who has difficulty responding emotionally. The light-heartedness which both Sally and Amabel share acts to complete Clarissa's and Miriam's reticence and carefulness. The overt expressions of love—Amabel's writing on the mirror and Sally's kiss—are impetuous and daring. Both girls are brave, independent; both have left home; yet each is extremely vulnerable. Ironically, marriage for both of them kills their spontaneity and creativity. Amabel becomes the suppressed, hard-worked wife and mother, her individuality submerged. Sally marries a rich man and has many sons. Clarissa remembers how Sally had "that quality which, since she hadn't got it herself, she always envied—a sort of abandonment, as if she could say anything, do anything; a quality much commoner in foreigners than in Englishwomen. Sally always said she had French blood in her veins" (p. 48). (So did Amabel—and she had that spontaneity of feeling popularly associated with the more "warm-blooded" French.) The word "abandonment" is the key here. Clarissa and Miriam admire the recklessness, freedom, lack of fear over loss of self, which these other women display.

This recklessness is also reflected in the character of Jinny in *The Waves*. She is the most physically expressive character whose consciousness is explored in Virginia Woolf's fiction; Sally Seton is only examined through the consciousness of others. Jinny's consciousness is filled with sense impressions, touch and smell in particular. She is always aware of her body. She tells us, "I do not dream" (p. 42). Instead she moves, dances; she dislikes words and communicates with her body. And her perceptions stop with her body: "I can imagine nothing beyond the circle cast by my body. My body goes before me, like a lantern down a dark lane, bringing one thing after another out of darkness into a ring of light" (pp. 128–29).

Isa in *Between the Acts* (1941)[21] also displays a great deal of awareness of movement in her consciousness:

> She returned to her eyes in the looking-glass. "In love," she must be; since the presence of his body in the room last night could so affect her; since the words he said, handing her a teacup, handing her a tennis racquet, could so attach themselves to a certain spot in her; and thus lie between them like a wire, tingling, tangling, vibrating—she groped, in the depths of the looking-glass, for a word to fit the infinitely quick vibrations of the aeroplane propeller that she had seen once at dawn at Croydon. Faster, faster, faster, it whizzed, whirred, buzzed, till all the flails became one flail and up soared the plane away and away. [Pp. 14–15]

Sexuality is associated with a great sense of movement in the consciousnesses of Virginia Woolf's women. And here it is especially fitting, if one remembers that Isa's consciousness reveals a preoccupation with the war, bombings, and brutality, to note that the images of sexual attraction in her mind are mechanical rather than organic.

To return to Clarissa, one discovers that she, like Miriam Henderson, experiences "love" for someone who resembles her own desired self. Clarissa says that Sally has a quality "she always envied." Envy turns to love rather than hostility, however, because the essential similarity of femininity allows for a communication which is not threatening. Envy she might feel for a man (over his freedom, education, physical power, etc.): that would admit a sense of inferiority and powerlessness. That kind of envy turns into defensiveness and hostility, and ultimately to rejection.

Additionally, the attraction for Sally allows Clarissa to utilize the masculine side of her consciousness, to reverse roles and *become*, if only for a brief moment, the feared and envied male. Orlando also has a moment when the sexual feelings of man and woman converge and become inseparable in consciousness. Since Orlando is completely androgynous, it is not merely imaginative identification, however. She really can react with "which is the

21. Virginia Woolf, *Between the Acts* (New York: Harcourt, Brace, 1941).

greater ecstasy? The man's or the woman's?"[22] and compare the differences by experience. "She was man; she was woman; she knew the secrets, shared the weaknesses of each" (p. 145).

But for Clarissa this shift in roles allows for an objectivity, a distance from which to worship her object of affection. To worship a male would place her in a subservient position where she might get hurt. To assume the male role and still worship allows her a sense of power and an absoluteness of feeling without loss of her self-esteem.

> The strange thing, on looking back, was the purity, the integrity, of her feeling for Sally. It was not like one's feeling for a man. It was completely disinterested, and besides, it had a quality which could only exist between women, between women just grown up. It was protective, on her side; sprang from a sense of being in league together, a presentiment of something that was bound to part them (they spoke of marriage always as a catastrophe), which led to this chivalry, this protective feeling which was much more on her side than Sally's. [P. 50]

Clarissa was able to express her feelings freely in this instance because that "presentiment" of their assured parting prevented her from the fear of losing—of being destroyed by giving up her self. Here she was able to feel completely and yet *not have to change her life*. To give up her self to Peter, for instance, would mean a lifetime of association and the chance for misery. Better not to give too much of the self if it is to be a permanent gift.

Sally's kiss she remembers as "the most exquisite moment of her whole life" (p. 52), associating it with images of "a diamond," "a present wrapped up, and told just to keep it, not to look at it" (p. 52), and "radiance," "revelation," and "the religious feeling" (p. 53). This is religious ecstasy when the subject and object are one—a moment of unity.

Another feature of Clarissa's relationship with men, which is of lesser significance perhaps than the preceding but is nonetheless important, is her maternalism. Again like Miriam Henderson, she is able to separate herself from men through gentle condescension. She refers to "her dear Peter at his worst; and he could be

22. Virginia Woolf, *Orlando* (London: Hogarth Press, 1928), p. 142.

intolerable; he could be impossible; but adorable to walk with on a morning like this" (p. 8), or to Richard and "his adorable, divine simplicity" (p. 182). Men, thus seen, are charming children, unsophisticated and easy to deal with.

Clarissa's maternal feelings surface in her protectiveness toward Peter, Richard, and Sally, as well as through her jealousy over Miss Kilman's influence upon her daughter Elizabeth. But the physical sensations of maternity are not part of Clarissa's consciousness in the novel. Bodily sensations are usually missing from her consciousness (except in the form of oblique images, or those sensations of pain I spoke about earlier). Much of this is related to her coldness, her growing absorption with consciousness rather than physicality. After all, Mrs. Dalloway is growing older, facing death. Yet, although it is apparent in Clarissa, it is a tendency not unique with her. An avoidance of physical relationships and *specific* descriptions of bodily sensations is general throughout Virginia Woolf's work (with the exceptions of a few passages in her novels).[23]

Physicality in the manner of Lawrence or Joyce is missing, and like Dorothy Richardson, Virginia Woolf seems to exclude whole areas from consciousness. Yet, conversely, she does give us characters who are aware of their bodies, and since her emphasis is on consciousness, body is only relevant in terms of its reflection in the mind. Of course Jinny is aware of herself totally through her bodily sensations (but even these are rather prudishly restricted to sensations of light and sound, movement, etc., and never explicit descriptions of sexual behavior).[24]

23. J. Oates Smith, "Henry James and Virginia Woolf: The Art of Relationships," *Twentieth Century Literature*, 10 (Oct., 1964), 126, contains some interesting comments on the lack of sexual passion in Woolf's novels.

24. Virginia Woolf's attitude toward explicit descriptions of sexuality may be surmised from her comments on Ernest Hemingway: "The greatest writers lay no stress upon sex one way or the other. The critic is not reminded as he reads them that he belongs to the masculine or the feminine gender. But in our time, thanks to our sexual perturbations, sex consciousness is strong, and shows itself in literature by an exaggeration, a protest of sexual characteristics which in either case is disagreeable. Thus Mr. Lawrence, Mr. Douglas, and Mr. Joyce partly spoil their books for women readers by their display of self-conscious virility; and Mr. Hemingway, but much less violently, follows suit. All we can do whether we are men or women, is to admit the influence, look the fact in the face, and so hope to stare it out of countenance" (in *Collected Essays*, II, 256).

But I don't want to overlook Susan in *The Waves,* whose consciousness is also centered in her body.[25] Susan mentions her physical appetites: "Now I am hungry" (p. 99). She says, "I am short. I have eyes that look close to the ground and see insects in the grass" (p. 15). But even though Susan's consciousness is centered in her body (and in the extensions of her body, her children and her possessions), she does not refer to her body very specifically. She speaks of her fertility but not the actual sensations of giving birth. She says at one point, "I am sick of the body" (p. 191), but that is part of a larger exhaustion: "Yet sometimes I am sick of natural happiness, and fruit growing" (p. 191).

Incidentally, there isn't an artist figure in Virginia Woolf's novels, with the exception of Orlando (who bears a son), who combines artistic creativity with maternity. Virginia Woolf implies that the two forms of creativity cancel each other out, a contention close to May Sinclair's conclusion in *The Creators.*

Clarissa must constantly deal with her own passivity; this is another facet of her "feminine consciousness." Perhaps this is why she so admires Sally's daring, and why she so fears Peter's forcefulness. At one point she becomes aware of Peter's opening his knife: "What an extraordinary habit that was, Clarissa thought; always playing with a knife. Always making one feel, too, frivolous; empty-minded; a mere silly chatterbox, as he used" (p. 65). The juxtaposition of the rather obviously Freudian symbol, the knife, with the reflection of passivity, "making one feel," illustrates her own uncertainty. Her feelings are not her own—he *made* her feel—and his power is contained within his "knife." At another point Clarissa reflects, "It was extraordinary how Peter put her into those states just by coming and standing in a corner. He

25. Jean Love explores the differences between the body awareness of Jinny and Susan: "Like Jinny in some respects and her antithesis in others, Susan is resolute, single-mindedly determined in choosing her mode of existence. Hers is also the life of the body, but of maternity more than sexuality. . . . Susan's self is fused with nature rather than with others, as is Jinny's self, and is only a partially differentiated object of contemplation. She thinks of self in relationship to nature and maternity and feels herself lived by nature. In her consciousness she becomes the things she sees and is identical with the seasons" (p. 215).

made her see herself; exaggerate" (p. 255). "Put her," "made her": here is repeated passivity.

External events affect her too; her consciousness is so open to influence in its relaxed state that she feels what happens is done to her rather than that she does anything to anyone. When she hears of Septimus's death, she responds with a statement of its effect on her: "Somehow it was her disaster—her disgrace. It was her punishment to see sink and disappear here a man, there a woman, in this profound darkness, and she forced to stand here in her evening dress" (p. 282). Now she is the passive recipient of the blows of fate. But her passivity in this sense is a result of her previous activity. The very next line is, "She had schemed; she had pilfered. She was never wholly admirable. She had wanted success. Lady Bexborough and the rest of it. And once she had walked on the terrace at Bourton" (p. 282).

Clarissa feels she must pay for any strivings, whether for success or for love. And in her recognition of this self-sacrifice (one might compare it with Mrs. Ramsay's same reaction), she becomes accepting and remarks next of her happiness, "It was due to Richard." The happiness comes through a *giving up of active striving*: "No pleasure could equal . . . this having done with the triumphs of youth, lost herself in the process of living, to find it, with a shock of delight, as the sun rose, as the day sank" (p. 282). Passive acquiescence to "the process of living" brings happiness; one must cease the struggle, the reactions against and for, the demands of the ego. And then, in imaginative identification with the dead Septimus (who lost himself completely), she remarks: "She felt somehow very like him—the young man who had killed himself. She felt glad that he had done it; thrown it away" (p. 283). Notice how she still admires recklessness! The ultimate passivity is in her recognition of the power of the dead man: "He *made* her feel the beauty; *made* her feel the fun" (p. 284; italics mine).

The irony of it all is that Clarissa achieves happiness not in maintaining an androgynous consciousness; that appears to be possible only for the artist and not for the ordinary woman who must complement her basic femininity with the masculinity of her partner, or with each of their masculine-feminine sides in proper balance with each other.[26] Clarissa's happiness seems to come when she is most passive, a traditionally "feminine" virtue. And that "femininity" for her too (as it was for Miriam Henderson and Mary Olivier) is ultimately sexless. With Mrs. Dalloway it takes the form of a growing understanding of her connections with all life—even in consciousness—and a giving up of the struggle to define her own consciousness or to hold it together and protect it from invasion.

IV   Although Clarissa Dalloway reveals androgynous elements in her consciousness, her femininity is much more obvious.[27] It might be helpful to analyze the concept further, then, in relation to a character whose androgyny is more essential than Clarissa Dalloway's, and one for whom androgyny is necessary for artistic creativity.[28] Certainly Orlando is the most completely androgynous character in her fiction, but, as J. B. Batchelor remarks, Virginia Woolf's focus is on her as "woman as writer rather than on woman as entity."[29] Orlando is part of a fantasy and is more a statement of ideas about sexuality, social attitudes, and literature than a character developed through her own consciousness. Lily Briscoe, however, is more relevant to a study of "feminine consciousness." She lives for the reader through her own consciousness (although, like Clarissa Dalloway and the others, correctives are established to her view of herself by providing statements made about her by other characters). And her consciousness, which

26. Herbert Marder comments on the need for complementary attributes in unifying a marriage with respect to Katherine Hilberry and Ralph Denham in *Night and Day* (1919): "Katherine and Ralph . . . are both essentially androgynous; each one combines the opposites within his own personality. But they are both vividly aware that a cleavage still exists between their practical lives and their dreams. To put it another way, the function of their marriage, both as symbol and as reality, is to enable them to complete each other, to help each other perfect their androgyneity" (p. 128).

27. Virginia Woolf's understanding of the androgynous grew out of her reading of Coleridge, where it was used to explain the mental bisexuality of great artists. See *A Room of One's Own* (New York: Harcourt, Brace, 1963), p. 102.

28. Marder considers Mrs. Ramsay "the androgynous artist in life, creating with the whole of her being" (p. 128).

29. Batchelor, p. 5.

contains a more equal balance of "masculine" and "feminine" tendencies, is also involved in the process of artistic creation.

Lily's androgyny is portrayed not only as the reflection of the ability to unify—to bring the different parts together—but also as the ability to use both of the capacities traditionally assigned to the sexes: intuition and reason. She has, in a very limited way, the capabilities Virginia Woolf noticed in Coleridge's description of the genius. Lily is far from a genius; she knows that her paintings will probably wind up in attics, but she still attempts to achieve unity of self through this most difficult process. In her struggle to complete her painting she tries to resolve the conflicts she feels about the Ramsay family and—by extension—the relationships between the male and the female, inside of consciousness and without.

Lily Briscoe is a woman who has probably been forced to forgo the usual route of marriage and children because of her physical deficiencies—plainness, lack of beauty. May Sinclair might have said that Lily's direction in life was determined by nature, but Virginia Woolf makes no such assertion. We are merely left with that underlying theme. It appears that Lily turned to art as sublimation. It is not really difficult to go even further and say that the primary factor in her androgyny is her sense of inferiority as a woman. Her relationship with Mrs. Ramsay, with all its ramifications of desire and hostility, envy and love, can only be resolved through some sort of impersonal conclusion. She must be able to separate herself from her feelings.[30]

Although Lily tries to remain separate from the emotions involved with family life, one need not accept her own explanation about why she did not marry as completely truthful. It is certain that she rejects the idea of marrying William Bankes, but perhaps she would not have rejected the idea of marrying someone younger, more sensual, and more assertively male. Lily's emotional responses differ from her conscious rationalization. For example, her attraction to Paul Rayley is only revealed in sudden moments when images from a deeper level of consciousness burst into her awareness. Toward the end of the novel, as Lily works toward

30. Marder, p. 56.

completion of her painting, she reflects upon Mrs. Ramsay and
her insistence that Lily marry. Lily feels proud that she won out
(and what a hollow victory it was!) by not falling under Mrs.
Ramsay's influence. Then, as Lily wonders about "this mania of
hers for marriage" (*To the Lighthouse*, p. 261), without warning
comes the following stream of images:

> (Suddenly, as suddenly as a star slides in the sky, a reddish light
> seemed to burn in her mind, covering Paul Rayley, issuing from
> him. It rose like a fire sent up in token of some celebration by
> savages on a distant beach. She heard the roar and the crackle.
> The whole sea for miles round ran red and gold. Some winey
> smell mixed with it and intoxicated her, for she felt again her
> own headlong desire to throw herself off the cliff and be drowned
> looking for a pearl brooch on a beach. And the roar and the
> crackle repelled her with fear and disgust, as if while she saw its
> splendour and power she saw too how it fed on the treasure of
> the house, greedily, disgustingly, and she loathed it. But for a
> sight, for a glory it surpassed everything in her experience, and
> burnt year after year like a signal fire on a desert island at the
> edge of the sea, and one had only to say "in love" and instantly,
> as happened now, up rose Paul's fire again. And it sank and she
> said to herself, laughing, "The Rayley's"; how Paul went to
> coffee-houses and played chess.) [Pp. 261–62]

The images of light and intoxication are associated with Paul
and being "in love." Her longing to throw herself recklessly into
the passion refers to the time, years ago, when she wanted to help
Paul find Minta's lost brooch. She wanted to be part of their
passionate love. The passage quoted above is set off from Lily's
conscious thoughts by its placement in parentheses. It is a single
explosion of imagery that occurs within a few seconds as part of
her longer sequence of thought, which includes rationalizations
over why she did not marry. Immediately after the violent image
passes, she has a reflection which tames the violence and alleviates
its painfulness: "She had only escaped by the skin of her teeth
though, she thought. She had been looking at the table-cloth, and
it had flashed upon her that she would move the tree to the mid-

dle, and need never marry anybody, and she had felt an enormous exultation. She had felt, now she could stand up to Mrs. Ramsay —a tribute to the astonishing power that Mrs. Ramsay had over one" (p. 262). Her decision not to marry was only directed at William Bankes and therefore was not an escape from passion, since there was no possibility of passion there. Paul Rayley was always an impossibility for her: young, handsome, in love with a beautiful girl. One must not forget Lily's homeliness. The sense of relief she expresses here, coming so soon after her spontaneous burst of emotional imagery, serves as self-deceptive consolation.

Lily's attraction for Paul is the most "feminine" part of her. The rest of her feelings are a mixture of desires and resentments, fundamentally ambivalent. She responds to Mrs. Ramsay with veiled hostility and painful longing. She is glad she triumphed over her by not marrying, but she also worships her and the ideal of femininity that she seems to represent. It is here that Lily's bisexuality is revealed.

So it is that on the one hand Lily resents Mrs. Ramsay's power and, since Mrs. Ramsay planned the Rayleys' marriage, is glad that the marriage is a failure. She considers that "Mrs. Ramsay has faded and gone. . . . We can override her wishes, improve away her limited, old-fashioned ideas" (p. 260). On the other hand, her feelings for Mrs. Ramsay contain elements of romance and love. Lily's bisexuality here grows out of her own sense of inadequacy when she compares herself to Mrs. Ramsay. This absorption of jealousy into passion for the object of envy is similar in some ways to the obsessions Miriam and Clarissa felt for their closest friends. But both of these women were more assured of their femininity than is Lily. Men fell in love with them, wanted to marry them. Lily never really has this kind of choice. For them, the passion for the other woman meant a completion of a feminine self rather than the agonized desire for loss of identity through worshipful identification. Lily's virginity is more complete, her purity, in the physical sense, far greater than Clarissa Dalloway's. Thus her love for Mrs. Ramsay is more painful. She not only loves Mrs. Ramsay and cannot express it, but she knows Mrs. Ramsay cannot return her love. And the love she feels goes further than Mrs. Ramsay herself to include the whole world that Mrs. Ramsay has created around her. In fact, there seems to be a suggestion that what Lily desires, ultimately, is an almost religious kind of communion with Mrs. Ramsay. Mrs. Ramsay's life seems to Lily so rich that she almost becomes a symbol of love and unification for her. In this way she is like a goddess, a knower, one who might have the answers Lily longs for.[31]

Part of Lily's pain must come, then, from her certainty that Mrs. Ramsay is incapable of understanding Lily's own life, which is so far from the beautiful fullness of her own. After all, "(. . . Mrs. Ramsay cared not a fig for her painting), or triumphs won by her (probably Mrs. Ramsay had had her share of those), and here . . . there could be no disputing this: an unmarried woman . . . has missed the best of life. The house seemed full of children sleeping and Mrs. Ramsay listening; shaded lights and regular breathing" (p. 77). The house with children sleeping contrasts with Lily's isolation. The passage which follows immediately elaborates Lily's rationalization of her own status and her attempt to maintain the purity of self—separateness—as she realizes it is better to worship from afar:

> Oh, but, Lily would say, there was her father; her home; even, had she dared to say it, her painting. But all this seemed so little, so virginal, against the other. Yet . . . gathering a desperate courage she would urge her own exemption from the universal law; plead for it; she liked to be alone; she liked to be herself; she was not made for that; and so have to meet a serious start from eyes of unparalleled depth, and confront Mrs. Ramsay's simple certainty (and she was childlike now) that her dear Lily, her little Brisk, was a fool. Then, she remembered, she had laid her head on Mrs. Ramsay's lap and laughed and laughed and laughed, laughed almost hysterically at the thought of Mrs. Ramsay presiding with immutable calm over destinies which she completely failed to understand. [Pp. 77–78]

31. Mythic elements in Mrs. Ramsay have been considered by Joseph Blotner, who views her as the "female principle of life" and associates her with the Greek goddesses of fertility ("Mythic Patterns in *To the Lighthouse*," *PMLA*, 71 (Sept., 1956), 547–62).

However, in spite of her doubts about Mrs. Ramsay's capacities for understanding, in spite of her own veiled resentment of the older woman, her need for Mrs. Ramsay is unabated:

> Was it wisdom? Was it knowledge? Was it, once more, the deceptiveness of beauty, so that all one's perceptions, half way to truth, were tangled in a golden mesh? or did she lock up within her some secret which certainly Lily Briscoe believed people must have for the world to go on at all? . . . Sitting on the floor with her arms round Mrs. Ramsay's knees, close as she could get, smiling to think that Mrs. Ramsay would never know the reason of that pressure, she imagined how in the chambers of the mind and heart of the woman who was, physically, touching her, were stood, like the treasures in the tombs of kings, tablets bearing sacred inscriptions, which if one could spell them out, would teach one everything. . . . What device for becoming, like waters poured into one jar, inextricably the same, one with the object one adored? Could the body achieve, or the mind, subtly mingling in the intricate passages of the brain? or the heart? Could loving, as people call it, make her and Mrs. Ramsay one? for it was not knowledge but unity that she desired. . . . [Pp. 78–79]

The phrase "not knowledge but unity that she desired" is crucial. Unity with Mrs. Ramsay herself is a hopeless dream. And the kind of unity within the self that Mrs. Ramsay was able to achieve is also beyond Lily's powers: "Mrs. Ramsay making of the moment something permanent (as in another sphere Lily herself tried to make of the moment something permanent)—this was of the nature of a revelation. In the midst of chaos there was shape; this eternal passing and flowing (she looked at the clouds going and the leaves shaking) was struck into stability" (p. 241). Mrs. Ramsay's power was to make life into art, Lily's to make art out of life. In order for Lily to do this, it is necessary for her to submerge her own particularized feelings, and also to submerge the completely feminine part of herself in order to achieve the kind of objectivity which is possible when the feminine vision (the possibility of seeing the essence of a moment, of synthesizing the whole intuitively rather than logically) is combined with masculine objectivity, distance from the object observed.

In order to make art out of life, Lily has to try to eliminate her own personal feelings of inferiority and uncertainty: "She took up once more her old painting position with the dim eyes and the absent-minded manner, subduing all her impressions as a woman to something much more general; becoming once more under the power of that vision which she had seen clearly once and must now grope for among hedges and houses and mothers and children—her picture. It was a question, she remembered, how to connect this mass on the right hand with that on the left" (pp. 82–83). The ultimate problem is to combine forces, to use both sides of her mind. This she cannot do when she is overwhelmed with the power of Mrs. Ramsay or caught up in sexual attraction for Paul Rayley. Batchelor has pointed out how Lily must withdraw in order to be an artist (as Clarissa must withdraw for completing her sense of self).[32] Withdrawal is necessary because creation involves such a tremendous upheaval of agonized self-doubting for Lily:

> It was in that moment's flight between the picture and her canvas that the demons set on her who often brought her to the verge of tears and made this passage from conception to work as dreadful as any down a dark passage for a child. Such she often felt herself—struggling against terriffic odds to maintain her courage; to say: "But this is what I see," . . . and so to clasp some miserable remnant of her vision to her breast, which a thousand forces did their best to pluck from her. [Note the implied image of mother holding a child to her breast to protect it from destructive forces.] And it was then too, in that chill and windy way, as she began to paint, that there forced themselves upon her other things, her own inadequacy, her insignificance. [P. 32]

Lily's certainty of vision is often threatened by any opportunity for criticism. Thus it is painful for her to have anyone look at her painting, for if anyone should criticize the validity of her point of view, that vision which she holds on to so uncertainly might collapse before her. She considers it "the awful trial of some one looking at her picture" (p. 80). Yet the possibility of developing intimacy with another—in this case William Bankes—is a result

32. Batchelor, p. 6.

of letting him look on and "see the residue of her thirty-three years" (p. 81). Moreover, since Lily fears intimacy even though she longs for it, she especially fears the criticism of the totally "masculine" mind, such as Tansley or Mr. Ramsay. She tries to avoid Mr. Ramsay's presence, for she fears that "any interruption would break the frail shape she was building" (p. 220). "But with Mr. Ramsay bearing down on her, she could do nothing. Every time he approached . . . ruin approached, chaos approached. She could not paint. . . . He made it impossible for her to do anything" (p. 221). Note Lily's essential passivity here: "He *made* it impossible." This is like Clarissa's reaction to Peter Walsh, but it goes even further: "Let him be fifty feet away, let him not even speak to you, let him not even see you, he permeated, he imposed himself. He changed everything" (p. 223).

Lily considers her own awareness of the effect of this kind of destructive critical presence on her in the following passage; this time it is in relation to Charles Tansley: ". . . why did she mind what he said? Women can't write, women can't paint—what did that matter coming from him, since clearly it was not true to him but for some reason helpful to him, and that was why he said it? Why did her whole being bow, like corn under a wind, and erect itself again from this abasement only with a great and rather painful effort?" (p. 130).

While in reaction to criticism she assumes a conventionally "feminine" pose of defensiveness and inferiority, Lily also reveals the obverse to this masochism once in a while. She thinks of Tansley then as "a whipping-boy." "She found herself flagellating his lean flanks when she was out of temper" (p. 293). Here again, an image from the depths of consciousness breaks out into the light and gives the reader an inkling of the submerged passions which cannot be realized in Lily's daily living.

Lily's androgynous consciousness is depicted in a number of ways. Yet the greatest testament to it is her capacity for imaginative identification with the mind of a man. Thus she can see "through William's eyes" (p. 264) and understand how he loves Mrs. Ramsay, not by guessing but by understanding her own love for the woman. The masculine part of her consciousness not only assumes the male role in loving, but it also has the ability to create images to fit those experiences. One discovers images in her consciousness that are conventionally masculine. Suitably, this imagery occurs when she considers the struggle involved in objectifying the moment. For, of course, the objectifying part of the task of creation belongs to the area of reason:

> Other worshipful objects were content with worship; men, women, God, all let one kneel prostrate; but this form, were it only the shape of a white lamp-shade looming on a wicker table, roused one to perpetual combat, challenged one to a fight in which one was bound to be worsted. Always (it was in her nature, or in her sex, she did not know which) before she exchanged the fluidity of life for the concentration of painting she had a few moments of nakedness when she seemed like an unborn soul, a soul reft of body, hesitating on some windy pinnacle and exposed without protection to all the blasts of doubt. [Pp. 236–37]

The image of combat, of fighting, of conquering an obstacle, draws out associations which are masculine. But the doubting, the unsureness, the voice echoing Tansley's "can't paint, can't write," are all illustrations of feminine insecurity.

Lily's "feminine consciousness" contains some of the other elements usually associated with femininity—at least some of those Miriam Henderson outlined for it in *Pilgrimage*. For one, it is remarkably concrete. She is more like Mrs. Ramsay when she concentrates on particularities rather than generalities. She always has her eye on the object. When she thinks about Mr. Ramsay's philosophizing, she sees "a scrubbed kitchen table" (p. 30). She must put Andrew's explanation of his father's work, "subject and object and the nature of reality," into specific terms. Thus she is always reminded of Andrew's hurried explanation, "Think of a kitchen table then . . . when you're not there" (p. 38). Or, in a slightly different context, she thinks sympathetically about Mr. Bankes, "You live for science (involuntarily, sections of potatoes rose before her eyes)"—again, a material object instead of an abstract concept.

But Lily is also capable of abstraction, very capable, and her ability comes from that rational side of her mind. But it displays a depth and sensitivity that may only be derived from a combination of that rationality with spontaneous insight. When she thinks further about Mr. Ramsay's work as a philosopher, she reflects, "Naturally, if one's days were passed in this seeing of angular essences, this reducing of lovely evenings, with all their flamingo clouds and blue and silver to a white deal four-legged table . . . naturally one could not be judged like an ordinary person" (p. 38). Her reflection contains a comment on the sterility of speculative thinking, "this reducing of lovely evenings." Ironically, her reference to those "angular essences" very closely describes her own method of painting. For Lily reduces the complexities of the Ramsays' life into triangular shapes and "lines running up and across" (p. 309). Here is an even more severe abstraction than Mr. Ramsay's, for hers is the freezing into form of the vital essence of the moment.[33]

The androgynous consciousness is made manifest through the unification of masculine and feminine principles into the creation of a work of art. It is a creation of consciousness rather than a creation of biology. Lily's "vision," like Clarissa's withdrawal, Miriam Henderson's "featureless freedom," and Mary Olivier's "secret happiness," is an isolated experience and an asexual one.[34]

33. See John Hawley Roberts, "Vision and Design in Virginia Woolf," *PMLA*, 61 (Sept., 1946), 842, for a comparison of Lily's ideas about art with those of Roger Fry.

34. John Edward Hardy comments upon the final desexualization in Lily's vision in "Vision without Promise," in *Man in the Modern Novel* (Seattle: University of Washington Press, 1964), p. 120.

Four

Rosamond Lehmann

AT THE center of Rosamond Lehmann's (1903–) treatment of feminine consciousness is the concept of "the source," what Sibyl Jardine in *The Ballad and the Source* (1944) refers to as "the quick spring that rises in illimitable depths of darkness and flows through every living thing from generation to generation. It is what we feel mounting in us when we say: 'I know! I love! I *am*!' "[1] The image of human being as vessel, as container for the life force—this is its application to woman as a physical being, as perpetuator of human existence. But in its connection with knowledge, the "I know" and the "I am," it refers to consciousness itself. And it is here that the metaphor of the stream becomes less effective when one considers Rosamond Lehmann's treatment of consciousness than with the others in this study. "The quick spring" is reminiscent of the Romantic image of the fountain. Out of a hidden and still source emerges with great energy, not of its own making, a powerful outpouring. Consciousness is not a stream but a finite collection of particles. In another place Rosamond Lehmann uses a perhaps unconsciously Jungian phrase when she refers to an "underground vat or generator with

1. Rosamond Lehmann, *The Ballad and the Source* (New York: Reynal & Hitchcock, 1945), p. 97.

which we are all equipped at birth—before our birth perhaps,"[2] which provides consciousness with its images.

In yet another context she links this storehouse of particles to the process of artistic creation, thus pulling together the Romantic notion of inspired vision with the Freudian concept of the unconscious: ". . . leisure employs me—weak aimless unsystematic unresisting instrument—as a kind of screen upon which are projected the images of persons—known well, a little, not at all, seen once, or long ago, or every day; or as a kind of preserving jar in which float fragments of people and landscapes, snatches of sound."[3] The writer is this preserving jar. And it is important to notice that she is *passive*. Power seems to be contained in the objects in the jar rather than in the jar itself. There is something organic about them; a dormant life is within them: "Yet there is not one of these fragile shapes and aerial sounds but bears within it an explosive seed of life. . . . Suddenly, arbitrarily one day, a spark catches, and the principle of rebirth contained in this cold residue of experience begins to operate. Each cell will break out, branch into fresh organisms. There is not one of them, no matter how apparently disconnected, that is not capable of combining with the rest at some time or another."[4]

If the artist is only a "preserving jar," one might ask then what accounts for talent? What differentiates the consciousness of the artist from that of the ordinary person? And the inescapable answer relates back again to that Romantic notion of genius that was mentioned earlier in connection with May Sinclair. Artistic creation becomes a spontaneous and primarily unconscious act. The artist has a gift which allows her to act as the catalyst for the creation of new life in the form of art. This theory implies the existence of an organic universe in which human beings share in the continual creation of newness. Since creation is spontaneous, being pulled out of the creator by forces not under her own control, the artist is, in a sense, passive:

2. Rosamond Lehmann, "Rosamond Lehmann Reading," in John Lehmann, "New Soundings," *New World Writing*, 2 (1952), 47.

3. Rosamond Lehmann, "The Red-Haired Miss Daintreys," *The Gipsy's Baby and Other Stories* (New York: Reynal & Hitchcock, 1946), p. 57.

4. *Ibid.*, pp. 57–58.

Yet when I come to think harder, it seems truer to say that the creator is *acted upon*: that what one really feels at the outset of the enterprise is: "This has started *to be done to me*." And that what is necessary is to remain as it were actively passive, with mind and senses at full stretch, incorporating, selecting, discarding; in fact abandoned—not to sanctimonious looseness—but to every unbargained-for, yet acceptable, inevitable possibility of fertilization.[5]

The writer, who is "acted upon," is open and ready for "every . . . possibility of fertilization." The inevitable comparison is, of course, with sexuality and procreation, and those from the feminine point of view. Rosamond Lehmann's aesthetic theory rarely strays from this basic analogy. In fact, the whole process of artistic production resembles the generative process. Thus she speaks of the novel as a work whose

> . . . genesis is the image, or isolated images which have become embedded in the mass of accumulated material in the author's "centre." When the moment comes (it cannot be predicted, but can be helped on by the right kind of passivity) these images will start to become pregnant, to illuminate one another, to condense and form hitherto unsuspected relationships. The characters will begin to emerge, to announce their names and reveal their faces, voices, purposes, and destinies. The author does not "invent" his characters or know about them from the outset. They reveal themselves gradually to him in and through that state of doubtful conviction which I have mentioned before. Characters must make plot or action; never the other way around.[6]

The author's characters, then, are created in spite of herself, much the same way that a baby grows within its mother, often against her own will. What makes these images "pregnant," what starts them out on their own, has something to do with a force outside will and invention. Coleridge's "secondary imagination" is perhaps the closest one comes to it.

Rosamond Lehmann illustrates the method of unconscious creation by showing how it was used by Virginia Woolf:

5. Lehmann, "Rosamond Lehmann Reading," p. 48.
6. Rosamond Lehmann, "The Future of the Novel," *Britain Today*, 122 (June, 1946), 9–10.

Virginia Woolf once told me that the primary image underlying her most complex novel *The Waves* was of a fin turning in
a waste of waters; and that the rhythmic pattern informing the
book's shape arose out of watching the flight of moths coming in
out of the night toward the lamp on her verandah. I thought and
still think that she was saying something of great importance
and fascination about the essential storing-house of the creative
writer: about the fluid territory, the seminal area within us, to
which we must return, in which we must immerse; but how to
do so, how not to destroy or be destroyed by its mysterious fer-
ments and fructifications; and then how to release and be released
by it, shape it and yet retain the tension in it, the reciprocity—that
is the heart of the matter that never can be learnt or taught by
textbook: any more than couples can discover marriage by studying those helpful little manuals of sex instruction; any more than
mothers can become mothers by proceeding as advised when
their infants object to spinach or the dark.[7]

Rosamond Lehmann's use here of a connection between creative
writing on the one hand, and sexuality and maternity on the other,
goes deeper than mere analogy. They all derive from the same
source, the unconscious. They are all unlearned *natural* functions.
The human being behaves (or rather should behave) in all three
instances, *intuitively*, responding to that inner source rather than
to rules or rationality.

What one discovers, then, in Rosamond Lehmann's novels is
a concept of consciousness which makes it a passive thing. It stores
memories and it responds to the *inherent* qualities in the stored
images and memories. Moreover, the passivity of consciousness is
paralleled by a passivity of behavior as well. Rosamond Lehmann's
characters are quite often "destroyed" by the "mysterious fer-
ments and fructifications" of their own consciousnesses as well as
by the forces of nature itself. How often the direction of one of
these novels changes because of the intrusion of nature—storms,
pregnancy, illness! In fact, these passive characters often seem
determined, both by the forces of nature within and without and
by their own stored past experiences. Like the images in the preserving jar of the author who evolved them, they contain little

7. Lehmann, "Rosamond Lehmann Reading," p. 47.

preserving jars of images and memories which cause them to respond to life in their characteristic ways.

But determinism in a Rosamond Lehmann novel is not the same as in one by May Sinclair. Missing is the nineteenth-century naturalism, the relentless course of heredity and environment. Missing also are the stereotyped Freudian case histories. Psychoanalytic concepts are apparent, especially regarding the unconscious, but those concepts are totally absorbed into the world view of these novels. They are part of the intellectual assumptions of the times and are not presented as theories to be expounded.

Yet although Rosamond Lehmann's approach to the novel is quite different from May Sinclair's—she does not write as a theorist or a philosopher—her place in this study is really quite similar. Like May Sinclair, Rosamond Lehmann is not really an innovator. May Sinclair drew upon the discoveries of Dorothy Richardson and simplified them, bringing the notion of "stream of consciousness" to a wider audience. Rosamond Lehmann, in turn, has followed Virginia Woolf and others, achieving a high degree of artistic success through the popularization of previously avant-garde techniques. Thus if one looks at her first novel, *Dusty Answer* (1927), and feels that it is the product of a more modern sensibility than Virginia Woolf's *To the Lighthouse*, which appeared the same year, still its modernity is revealed through its outspoken treatment of sexuality rather than by any advance in technique. In terms of technical experimentation *Dusty Answer* is decidedly old-fashioned. In fact, Rosamond Lehmann continues to be technically conservative throughout her career. This conservatism is exemplified by her late use of the internal monologue in *The Weather in the Streets* (1936) and the Jamesian study in point of view in *The Ballad and the Source* (1944). Her most experimental novel, *The Echoing Grove* (1953), uses some of the aspects of multiple consciousnesses which Virginia Woolf worked out in *Mrs. Dalloway* before 1925.

Nevertheless, although Rosamond Lehmann might not have created a new method of exploring the feminine consciousness, she has certainly expanded and deepened the concept. Feminine consciousness is brought back to its connection with the sexuality of women—to its physical as well as spiritual basis. Her precise psychological penetration of women prevents them from ever becoming abstracted symbols, as do those in Virginia Woolf's *The Waves*. This is primarily a difference in technique, but it also suggests a different starting point. Rosamond Lehmann's novels present women realistically and deal with the condition of being female. They are usually about women caught up in their inter-actions with men and with other women and with children. For Rosamond Lehmann, "The basis of the novel is after all personal relationships."[8] Thus the consciousnesses of her women are usu-ally focused on themselves in relation to other people rather than to any abstract principle, either of art or religion. Her own remarks on Virginia Woolf suggest the essential distinction between them: "It is true that there was much she lacked, much which was out-side the scope of her powers. She was not equipped for a broad grasp of humanity, she had not the kind of richness and sanity, the rooted quality which comes from living a completely fulfilled life as a woman and a mother."[9] That "rooted quality" she found lacking in Virginia Woolf is at the foundation of her own writing and, in fact, may be considered the basis for her interpretation of feminine consciousness.

II   Feminine consciousness in Rosamond Lehmann's novels
        is directly related to the biological condition of femaleness, and as a result, the women in these novels seem to live more com-pletely within their bodies than do those of the earlier authors in this study. They admire themselves, worry about their figures or faces, eat or forget to eat, suffer illness, and—most essential—experience pregnancy and childbirth. Their feminine conscious-nesses are definitely connected with their physical beings and the sexual nature of femininity. The meaning, the purpose, the goal of life often appears related to the achievement of the right re-lationship with the male—or, going beyond that, of the relation-ship with one's children. Intellectual achievement, political in-

8. Lehmann, "The Future of the Novel," p. 8.
9. Rosamond Lehmann, "For Virginia Woolf," *Penguin New Writing*, 7 (June, 1941), 57.

volvement, artistic creation, even "self-fulfillment" in such terms as independence, all seem to be eventually subordinated to that overwhelming urge for union with the male and procreation. This is not to say that her women hide themselves away in seclusion from the world. Not at all. They participate in the activities of the world, and not with the kind of either/or tension of May Sinclair's intellectual women who decide not to marry in order to be free or to have careers. Rosamond Lehmann's women are able to take part in the world and create without forgoing sexual experience. But it does appear that whatever else they may be doing is overshadowed by the demands of their emotional lives, as, when Olivia in *The Weather in the Streets* considers the change in herself since falling in love, she says, "What happened to the person I was beginning to know before."[10]

Except for Dinah in *The Echoing Grove*[11] and Mrs. Jardine in *The Ballad and the Source,* her major characters do not attempt to be intellectuals or feminists. Judith of *Dusty Answer* (1927)[12] and Olivia of *Invitation to the Waltz* (1932)[13] and *The Weather in the Streets* (1936) are sensitive, imaginative, and poetic but not scholarly or committed to any particular vocation. If one compares Olivia's life as a single woman in London with Miriam Henderson's in Dorothy Richardson's *Pilgrimage,* one finds none of the latter's enthusiasm, fascination with the urban panorama, and exultation in independence. For Olivia it is less a matter of choice than necessity—a round of parties, an uninspiring job, a period of waiting to be gotten through. She needs a man to make her life worthwhile, and her unfortunate love affair with the married Rollo Spencer does not satisfy because she needs permanent protection.

The attitude of the women in Rosamond Lehmann's novels toward their own bodies is particularly important. Judith in *Dusty*

10. Rosamond Lehmann, *The Weather in the Streets* (New York: Reynal & Hitchcock, 1936), p. 156.

11. Rosamond Lehmann, *The Echoing Grove* (New York: Harcourt, Brace & World, 1953).

12. Rosamond Lehmann, *Dusty Answer* (New York: Henry Holt, 1927).

13. Rosamond Lehmann, *Invitation to the Waltz* (New York: Henry Holt, 1932).

Answer is aware of a sensual relationship between her body and nature. For example, during her nude swim early in the novel: "The water was in love with her body. She gave herself to it with reluctance and it embraced her bitterly. She endured it, soon she desired it; she was in love with it" (p. 53). She admires her body because it is in harmony with nature. But that harmony is a fragile one dependent upon her youth, beauty, illusions, and inexperienced sexuality. Her attitude toward her body here is in keeping with her adolescent frame of mind, which is romantic and narcissistic. Nature and body reflect each other, love each other.

Judith accepts this connection between her body and nature because she has not yet been introduced to that condition where the will of nature becomes other than her own desires. Disharmony between conscious desires and nature is apparent, however, when body and mind are in opposition, as when Olivia becomes pregnant in *The Weather in the Streets*.

The absolute importance of Olivia's pregnancy to herself is illustrated by Rosamond Lehmann's technique in describing it. Olivia's first intimations of pregnancy occur on the train back to England after a vacation in Austria with her lover. In the very last section of Part II (which describes the affair through Olivia's first-person point of view, although in retrospect), the time shifts to the present and Olivia begins to worry about her missed menstrual period:

> . . . Six, seven days late....I'm worried. But it's happened once before, the first year Ivor and I were married; over a week then, I was beginning to be sure—but it was a false alarm....That was in August too—so I expect it's the time of year, I'm sure I've heard it does happen sometimes: or all that long cold bathing, lake water's very cold, that might easily account for it....I'm worried. Falling for one, Mrs. Banks calls it. "When I fell for our Doris...." I feel a bit sick. Train-sick, I expect. I've never been train-sick in my life. This morning when I got up, suddenly retching as I began to wash....Nerves. Lying down like this I feel fine. Be all right tomorrow. Sleep. Thank God for lying down, a sleeper to myself. . . .
> Switch on the blue light. No, off again—too mournful. The

water-bottle rattles. Is the stopper out?—The cupboard door un-
latched? My hands are dry, I feel the smuts in my nails....

Queer, how a train journey throws up images, applies some
stimulus to memory and desire....

The story unrolled from the beginning in a kind of rough
sequence; like when a person's drowning, so they say...

Ai, what a screech....Into a tunnel, my ears thicken...out again.
Nearer home, nearer Rollo. Tomorrow, come quick...don't come.
...Slowing down now. . . .

Relax, go with the train's speed, give to its swaying....Breathe,
breathe easily....

Sleep.... [Pp. 245–46]

The passage represents the speeded-up thinking typical during
emotional disturbance. But although it resembles "stream of consciousness," it really is a much more limited and abstracted internal monologue. The thoughts form logically related sequences,
not free association; all the thoughts refer to the one central issue.
Bodily sensations, memories, analysis, all belong to the fear of
pregnancy. There is not the disjunction one finds in a complete
representation of stream of consciousness, nor does one find the
often incongruous imagery of synaesthesia. Instead, the physical
sensations are sharp and distinct. Olivia is bothered by the light,
hears noises, notices minute details.

The overriding feeling in the passage is denial. Olivia tries to
blame her sensations on the cold water, train-sickness, nerves. But
the seemingly incongruous reference to Mrs. Banks calling it
"falling for one" indicates that deeper in her consciousness she
knows the reason for her sickness. Not only does she know, but
subconsciously her choice of the old-fashioned phrase "falling
for one"—so out of keeping with her own sophisticated jargon—
points out her real attitude toward the event and its cause. Subtly,
the guilt over her illicit relationship surfaces in an image of falling
down, of slipping, of being punished.

As pregnancy becomes an obvious fact, Olivia's supersensitivity
to objects and sense impressions worsens: "Etty's jasmine soap
reached her nostrils in greasy nauseating whiffs. Why does everything smell as if it's gone bad" (p. 255). Denial and rejection work

on her thinking: "Nothing revives me, nothing freshens me. My body is loathsome" (p. 256). Even more important is Olivia's turning against Rollo, the necessary second party to her predicament: ". . . Get hold of Rollo. But I don't want to...I don't want to see him or think of him. How can this be, in twenty-four hours? Is it a symptom, does it seal my fate?...The female, her body used, made fertile, turning, resentful, in hostile untouchability, from the male, the enemy victorious and malignant....Like cats or bitches...Ugh!" (p. 249).

Anger at being used, at being taken over by forces of nature, turn her against Rollo. It is an insult to her self-determination. And in her consciousness she summons up images of animals to associate herself with others like her. The world of nature is becoming more a reality than the world of society. Thus, as nature takes her over, Olivia's conditioned responses to the world of objects changes. She experiences them all as if they were new, and instead of producing their old reactions in her, they cause her to experience nausea. What this means is that she has become unable to accept whatever is outside her own body and must reject it. She finds that she cannot wear bright colors or smell certain odors. She is focused on food; she might desire cheese or a lamb cutlet. She wants to be cared for, fed. She feels she is "lowering herself unresistingly to a vegetable standard: A maggotty spoiling vegetable" (p. 293).

Pregnancy for Olivia is a sickness, a reversion to an animal—even a vegetable—state. After her abortion she thinks, "I can be human and have thoughts again" (p. 327). Evidently, to be human is not to be pregnant. It implies the ability to think and the ability to control physical cravings like those for food. It means being able to experience external reality without nausea. Olivia's feminine consciousness rejects her body's natural function. But at the same time it is rejecting something that she wants on a deeper level: Rollo's child. That is natural, the result of love. But the complications of social life and her feared rejection by Rollo are what affect her ability to accept her nature.

Dinah in *The Echoing Grove* shares with Olivia guilt over an illicit affair. She also runs into trouble with child-bearing, but she wants her child. She likes to fantasize its future and her life with it. In this case, however, the child is born dead, delivered incorrectly by a friend in the midst of an unexpected storm. Looking back on her realization that her baby was born dead, Dinah thinks: "... I realized there was a moment about half-way through when the intimation reached me that...something biding its time from the beginning had stepped from ambush and taken charge. The enterprise was moving to its predestined outcome. But one is never prepared for what one has prepared to bring about" (pp. 36–37).

III   It is one thing to recognize one's affinity with nature, to know that one is caught up in an unrelenting cycle of growth and decay, and quite another thing to accept it. Rosamond Lehmann's women frequently attempt to step outside the cycle and freeze experience where it is. They fear change. This is true even for the adolescent Judith of *Dusty Answer*; for example, after an unusually beautiful day she hopes, "If only the moment could stay fixed, if their strange and thoughtful faces could enclose her safely for ever in their trance of contentment" (pp. 97–98). It is even truer of Grace Fairfax in *A Note in Music* (1930).[14] Grace remembers one perfect day in her life: "And as she lay watching, all had become fixed, crystallized into forms absolute and eternal. Earth and sky mirrored each other in a blue element half air, half water" (p. 38).

But Grace differs from Judith in that her attempt to freeze experience implies a rejection of emotional life; it is an attempt to stop the flow of time by nonparticipation. As a result, she has slipped into a premature middle age through her inability to throw herself into life: "She saw an old self in a flash: an even-tempered young married woman with a hopeful outlook and the average activities of her kind. What in the world could have happened to her?...It was all her own fault, for she had no troubles, no real ones. It must be that she had been too unspiritual to keep a young heart; she had allowed the years, like a slow and fleshy vegetable growth, to stifle her. It was her own fault" (pp. 26–27).

14. Rosamond Lehmann, *A Note in Music* (London: Chatto & Windus, 1930).

Judith's desire to escape from the flux of life is only temporary, however. She still has what Grace called "a young heart." Judith reflects that "there was value in impermanence, in insecurity; it meant an ache and quickening, a perpetual birth; it meant you could never drift into complacence and acceptance and grow old" (*Dusty Answer*, p. 150).

The acceptance of impermanence—a far more difficult reaction to life than denial—allows for brief moments of timelessness. When lost in their passions, these women became unconscious participants in universal movement. Grace Fairfax recognizes this condition after it has passed, after her brief awakening to sexual passion: "Never again would she be dissolved, poured through the universe with the insubstantial elements of light and colour, reunited with the component forces of vital energy" (*A Note in Music*, p. 296).

Rosamond Lehmann's women view love as an almost mystical experience which is part of a determined cycle. Dinah's remark about the "predestined outcome" is one part of it. Love is the agent which allows these women to become a part of what is uncontrollable, unstable, and vital. Its impermanence makes for its intensity. Dinah's dead baby might be representative of the dark side, as is Olivia's unwanted pregnancy with its retreat and withdrawal. But the other side is the joy of involvement. The most appealing characters in these novels let themselves get caught up in these life processes; nature works upon them, and they are open to it.

Olivia's readiness to give herself up to love is foreshadowed in an earlier novel, *Invitation to the Waltz* (1932), where she is shown as a young girl attending her first dance. This seemingly simple yet technically complex novel is written in the third person, but Olivia's point of view is really its center. It is a story of an awakening, a brief moment of surprise and pleasure at the richness of human experience and the wonders of existence. Olivia lives her first dance totally, even though she does not realize her imagined goals of romance and attention. She ponders the meaning of the dance, curious that she feels satisfied: "I've had a lot really, one way and another. What was it that, at the last, had made almost a richness? Curious fragments, odds and ends of looks, speeches" (p. 298). At the close of the novel she runs out into the fields on the morning after the dance. Suddenly, breathlessly, she sees: ". . . A winged gigantic runner with a torch was running from a great distance to meet her, swooping over the low hills, skimming from them veil after veil of shadow, touching them to instant ethereal shapes of light. On it came, over ploughed field and fallow. The rooks flashed sharply, the hare and his shadow swerved in sudden sunlight. In a moment it would be everywhere. Here it was. She ran into it" (pp. 308–9).

Olivia has been given quite a few blows by the winged runner by the time she appears again, in her late twenties, in *The Weather in the Streets*. She has been married, separated, and lives poorly in a semi-Bohemian, Depression London. But her essential vitality wells up again, and she seems bound to run toward that winged runner once more. This time it appears in the shape of a charming, but weak, married man and an affair that is doomed to fail from the start. This novel effectively illustrates a characteristic Simon Raven pointed out when he said that there is an implied question —"*Was it worth it?*"—in all her novels: "You didn't...you couldn't ...win but you did have the ecstasy of the game: does this compensate you for the pain and humiliation of the ultimate defeat?"[15] Raven comments on the relentlessness of the pursuit of love in *The Weather in the Streets*: ". . . love between human beings is now the *only* thing; it must be followed wherever it calls, it will lead to hideous disaster, and this serves us right because we are unworthy."[16]

Eventually, it is their underlying belief that they are unworthy that is revealed in the tragedies of these women: the abortion, the death of a baby, or the loss of a son in war. But in the moments when they ignore the possible future ramifications of their actions, when they are giving themselves to "the ecstasy of the game," they are at their best.

Olivia demonstrates this state of completeness during her first

15. Simon Raven, "The Game That Nobody Wins: The Novels of Rosamond Lehmann," *London Magazine*, 3 (Apr., 1963), 61.
16. *Ibid.*, p. 63.

sexual encounter with Rollo: ". . . just then it didn't seem particularly important to arrange for our next meeting: everything would glide on without our worrying and be all right....It's strange how incurious, unpossessive we both were then. It might have finished that night. It might have been enough...or couldn't it have been really?" (*The Weather in the Streets*, p. 168). Before the need to solidify, to possess, to freeze experience overcomes her, Olivia is spontaneous and full. Yet maintaining a relationship on the free basis of its beginning becomes impossible. Olivia knows she cannot maintain that spontaneity; it has lost its essence because it is forced. And then she discovers that the relationship really exists without any proper connections with the rest of her life: "Searching back into that time, it seems confused with hiding, pretence and subterfuge and covering our tracks...though it didn't seem to matter then. But now I see what an odd duality it gave to life: being in love with Rollo was all important, the times with him the only reality; yet in another way they had no existence in reality" (p. 173). She recognizes eventually the weakness of a relationship based on moments separated from all others: "Nothing stays without development, growth or decay. The pause has gone on too long, the immobility....Like August, the sinister pause in the year....But August will go over, the year tip imperceptibly towards inevitable change" (pp. 238–39).

Along with an awareness of change and the pained longing to halt it runs a preoccupation with memory in many of these women's consciousnesses, what an early critic of Rosamond Lehmann called "the perilous enchantment of things past."[17] Olivia, for example, contrasts a moment of happiness in childhood with the disillusionment of her present life, where she and Rollo "hung separated, cold and light—hollow people" (p. 136). She remembers days of bicycling and picnicking, climbing and eating candy bars, and reflects: "All that was important: had made an experience of emotion more complex, penetrating and profound, yes, than getting married" (p. 137). Olivia, like other female characters in Rosamond Lehmann's novels, turns back to childhood,

17. George Dangerfield, "Rosamond Lehmann and the Perilous Enchantment of Things Past," *Bookman*, 76 (Feb., 1933), 172–76.

through the medium of memory, in order to hold onto a moment of wholeness. The world of childhood remains uncorrupted, a time of innocence. In one of her short stories a woman reflects, ". . . This pure goodwill and disinterestedness of children, this concentration of spirit so entire that they seemed to fuse with and become the object, lifted her on a cool wave above her sickness, threw her up in a moment of absolute peace, as after love or child-birth upon a white and abstract shore."[18]

A brief excursion into the past through memory may give a character some temporary relief from the present, yet she usually emerges from it unsatisfied. Nora McKay, Grace's friend in *A Note in Music*, meditates upon the workings of time on the memory:

> It does not ease the burden of the past to share its recollections; for with each plunge into it, each withdrawal, something is left behind that weighs more heavily than the memory; something that can never be shared or imparted—a sense of accumulating unease, surprise and contrast, of going alone, in unsuspected iso-lation, on one's way; and worse, a comfortless suggestion that the way—life, in fact—is without continuity. . . . No, as one rushes headlong, flying with Time, portions of life split off and float away, one little world after another; and looking back, one sees them behind one as stars and constellations. Old burning pieces of experience shine now from their fixed places with unimpas-sioned ray; perhaps that fragment torn apart with cruellest wrench and most shattering concussion now hangs there, close indeed, but cold, all fires extinct, like that dead star the moon. . . .
>
> Yet, though one never can recapture . . . there come now and then—at a sound, a scent, a word—intimations from the past; live threads waver out, throwing feelers after hints of affinity. Misgiving comes, bewilderment, hope, surmise—a host of wit-nesses, striving to shape the spiritual shape of what has been; till it seems in a moment all will be linked, gathered up into unity and purpose. And the moment does not come, or comes too briefly, too dubiously to seize; and at length the whirling pace is slackened, the fires grow feebler; they flicker and pause, diminu-tive in the void; they have vanished. [Pp. 76–77]

18. Rosamond Lehmann, "A Dream of Winter," in *The Gipsy's Baby*, p. 107.

The desire to pull everything together, to make sense of it all as a unity of experience—all aspects of which are necessarily linked together—is the goal. If life must exhibit change, if pain is inevitable in the nature of it, let it at least have *meaning*. This seems to be the plea that runs through all the feminine consciousnesses in these novels. But the insistence on meaning conflicts with the possibility of its occurring. The title of Rosamond Lehmann's first novel reflects the basic theme:

> Lovers beneath the singing sky of May,
> They wandered once; clear as the dew on flowers:
> But they fed not on the advancing hours:
> Their hearts held cravings for the buried day.
> Then each applied to each that fatal knife,
> Deep questioning, which probes to endless dole.
> Ah, what a dusty answer gets the soul
> When hot for certainties in this our life!—
> George Meredith, *Modern Love*

The need for certainty, the quest for truth, runs counter to the experience of the moment. Life offers wonder and beauty, but they must be accepted for what they are: temporal, ephemeral.

Moments of illumination, then, figure prominently in these novels. Life in general is seen by these women as inevitably painful and ultimately disastrous; but living is worth it because of those moments. They reflect the intuitive, uncategorical side of the feminine consciousness described by Dorothy Richardson and Virginia Woolf. But Rosamond Lehmann uses them slightly differently. They are not so much moments of communion with the universe as moments of clear insight into the truth of a situation, more like epiphanies. One of the best examples occurs when Olivia has an almost psychic, immediate recognition that Rollo's wife is pregnant. This knowledge comes to her while she and Rollo stand watching the river, ducks, and swans, during a magnificent sunset:

> "Look!"
> It was seeing too much. She turned away her head and looked at him instead.
> What's to come next?

Oh, I see!...An illumination went through her, sharp, piercing and gone again: what I've been waiting for. All the pieces fell together...like the broken-up bits in James' kaleidoscope we used to look through, exclaiming at the patterns.

"Oh, I see...."

She was scarcely aware of saying it aloud until she saw his unconscious lips move, murmuring some vague word of query or endearment.

But it's nothing to do with him....We are born, we die entirely alone: I've seen how it will be. To suffer such dissolution and resurrection in one moment of time was an experience magnificent enough in itself. It was far above the level even of the lake, the chestnuts. It should have no sequel.

Everything went away again....There it is: a fact in the world that must be acted on. . . . [Pp. 359–60]

Olivia's moment of insight combines an intuition about Rollo with a deeper one about her own—and others'—condition: "We are born, we die entirely alone."

IV   The passivity of the creative artist is analogous to the passivity of most of the major characters in Rosamond Lehmann's novels. Although her women are not always true to the myth of sexual passivity (in that they often are aggressive in pursuit of the male), they are indeed passive in a larger sense. If one considers their own interior views of the world and their own behavior in it, one finds that they *see* themselves as passive creatures, their consciousnesses reveal them as receivers of action rather than initiators. Mrs. Jardine is the striking exception; she acts. But the reader does not penetrate her consciousness to discover how she views her own behavior. With the women whose consciousnesses are explored, however, passivity is a dominant characteristic.

Female passivity is communicated in several ways. At its simplest level one finds the passivity of the listener. The child Rebecca *receives* the bizarre story of passion and madness from several other characters in *The Ballad and the Source* (1944). Her consciousness is used as a passive medium for the communication of the various aspects of the tale. The preserving-jar image is relevant here also, because Rebecca *stores* the many details of the story. But she cannot grasp its underlying meaning through any rational attempt at putting the contradictory pieces together. It is only when the subconscious—that preserving jar—acts without her control through the medium of a dream, forming from those fragments a dream of terror, that the true meaning is made clear to Rebecca. One must remember that she does not consciously form this final interpretation of the events. In fact, it goes counter to her conscious defense of Mrs. Jardine. In her dream, welling up from the deepest level of her consciousness, Rebecca sees Mrs. Jardine watching her, blue hood over her head, and perceives the woman's malignance. She wakes in terror.

The second level of passivity is that of observer. In *Invitation to the Waltz* Olivia watches the activity of the dance. Her participation is based on her physical presence and on her extreme sensitivity. People *use* her because she seems so defenseless. The unhappy Peter can use her to vent his hostility against society rather than directly attack the people who upset him. Olivia receives not only hostility, however, but confidences—sly glimpses at the subtle workings of a large social event—so that through her sympathetic openness, which draws out these confidences, she receives more from the dance than anyone else there. In fact, the whole dance is, in a sense, possessed by her, since it lives for the reader through her eyes. By way of contrast, her sister Kate's experience is more limited, if more intense. Her view is entirely limited by her focus on Tony and romance. Olivia is open to everything and everybody—young, old, sad, happy. She reacts to what comes to her. That is why her final moment in the novel when she runs out to meet that winged runner—Life—is so fitting. Olivia opens herself to receive whatever comes.

The third and most relevant level of passivity is the role as woman. In line with these women's acceptance of their natural sexual function (as mothers, lovers of men), and their attitudes about time and nature discussed previously, one discovers a submissiveness, a sense of self-sacrifice as well. This is particularly true of the female characters who are mothers. The impingement upon their freedom by the responsibilities of their families, the demands of their husbands, occupies a large place in their consciousnesses. Nora MacKay in *A Note in Music* muses:

> Why should this vampire family so prey on her and pin her down that even one afternoon's freedom became a matter of importance, to be regretted afterwards? Why should she let him for ever drain her to sustain himself? [P. 52]

Immediately following her complaint, however, comes her acceptance:

> . . . It was no virtue in her, but a law of nature. To grudge him what she had within her to give him was as if one born with the power of healing by the laying-on of hands should refuse the sick a life-giving touch.
>
> Electricity, vitality, spirit—call it what you would—the supply was not to be exhausted by one demand, however ravenous and perennial. . . . Only, to-night she hated the active life, wanted to have rest from this perpetual crumbling of the edges, this shredding out of one's personality upon minute obligations and responsibilities. She wanted, even for a few moments, to feel her own identity peacefully floating apart from them all, confined and dissolved within a shell upon which other people's sensibilities made no impression. But this was not possible, never for a second, in one's own home. [Pp. 52–53]

The phrase "this shredding out of one's personality upon minute obligations and responsibilities" is reminiscent of Mrs. Ramsay in *To the Lighthouse* (as is a picture of Olivia's mother knitting in *Invitation to the Waltz*, p. 115). Behind this is the concept of woman as the source of life. Mrs. Jardine's ecstatic glorification of the concept in the passage quoted at the beginning of this chapter is the most explicit statement of it. Incidentally, Rebecca's reaction to Mrs. Jardine's description of "the fount of life" is of "a flying vision of streams and fountains, and myself borne along, dissolved in their elemental welling-up and flow" (p. 97). Her passive, subconscious understanding of the concept shows it to be itself a matter of a passive going-along-with nature.

But Mrs. Jardine's glorification of the "source" is ironic, for as Vida Marković points out, with her "the waters that spring from the source are grim and troubled. They cannot nourish new life and give it the vitality it needs to survive unscathed the pains of growth to which every living being is exposed."[19]

The demands upon the "source"—that is, upon the maternal figure—are at odds with individuality in many cases. A conflict similar to the one May Sinclair outlined in *The Creators* (1910) marks Mrs. Jardine. Her conflict, however, is not revealed through her own consciousness but is only hinted at through some of her speeches. Marković describes her as "an arche-type of a central human experience, that of the woman—a mother in this instance —who has not been cast for the part she is required to play." Sibyl Jardine is "a talented, even brilliant woman whose assumption of motherhood poisons her being."[20]

Mrs. Jardine's rejection of her child is followed by the birth of her ardent feminism. But she is divided between her guilt and obsessive longings for her daughter and the demands of her own individualism. Mrs. Jardine is the most outspoken feminist (and, revealingly, one of the least likable women) in Rosamond Lehmann's fiction. The others express the problem of being a woman with less hostility and more resignation. They appear to have accepted the submissive role in one way or another.

Submissiveness is frequently dishonest, a way of manipulating others. Thus one sees Olivia pretending to be interested in hunting to make herself pleasing to her dance partner (*Invitation to the Waltz*, p. 215). Or take the case of Judith in *Dusty Answer*. Judith, more rebellious than the adolescent Olivia, briefly accepts a conventional male-female relationship. She is aware that her partner "loved to have her beside him, behaving nicely and looking pretty, shewing interest, and smiling when it was seemly" (p. 283).

Judith fools herself here, and in a moment of utter passivity she imagines the only ideal form possible for this unseemly match: "If only their marriage could be a perpetual sitting on a green bank by a stream, watching him tolerantly, almost tenderly, with a quiet pleasure in his bodily magnificence . . . while her mind was

19. Vida E. Marković, "Mrs. Jardine," in *The Changing Face: Disintegration of Personality in the Twentieth-Century British Novel* (Carbondale: Southern Illinois University Press, 1970), p. 98.
20. *Ibid.*, p. 99.

off on its own, worlds removed from him!" (p. 283). How similar this all is to Miriam Henderson's reaction to Densley: someone who will not tamper with her mind, someone who will adore her, pay her homage, yet allow her inner freedom because he is incapable of understanding her. But that freedom is paid for by isolation.

V   Some of the dishonesty and deceptiveness which these women reveal stems from their recognition of their own powerlessness. They are women in a world dominated by men and masculine values and concepts. As corrupted as Sibyl Jardine becomes, one senses that the corruption had grown out of her early recognition of the unfair relationship between men and women, and her development of a defensive egotism strong enough to allow her to break away from what was expected of her. She is convincing when she tries to inspire the preadolescent Rebecca with her hopes for the future: "One day, Rebecca, women will be able to speak to men—speak out the truth, as equals, not as antagonists, or as creatures without independent moral rights—pieces of men's property, owned, used and despised . . ." (*The Ballad of the Source*, p. 97). The feminism of the old woman, hard and embittered, finds a ready audience in the child who worships her. Rebecca already has a sense of injustice owing to her sex; her baby brother is left a legacy, while she and her two sisters are forgotten: "He, Boy, sprawling at ease, without care or conscience in his perambulator, had casually tossed in the claim of male superiority and bagged the lot. Sylvia had voiced the feelings which our own years forbade, or took at least the sting from, when she bitterly remarked, the morning the news broke: 'I bet I was never called Girl when I was a baby!' " (p. 200).

Rebecca, born into the same male-dominated, pre–World War I society which Sibyl Jardine rebelled against, will grow up in a world where the differences between the sexes have narrowed. Like Judith, Olivia, and Dinah, her years of maturing are postwar. In fact, all of Rosamond Lehmann's women experience difficulties with the opposite sex because of the wide disparity between what they were brought up to believe in as femininity or masculinity and the real conditions of modern life. They are caught up in a feminine consciousness that relates only to an old reality.

The masculine ideal of Judith's childhood was Charlie. He represented the type of manhood—strong, beautiful, intelligent, and whole—which predated the war. But he was killed. The men who come later seem in contrast either simpler (Martin), or more hostile (Julian), or neurotic (Roddy). Judith cannot focus her passions on Martin because he is too different from her, nor on Julian because he is too cynical. But Roddy, in his remote, alienated, and helpless way, engages both her maternalism and her narcissism. Unable to accept the old pattern of male dominance, female submission (except in those few moments of escape with Martin, which I discussed earlier), she chooses someone with whom she foresees some kind of possible communion. Unfortunately her choice is the wrong one; Roddy is incapable of returning her affection. In choosing the man who most resembles herself, she chooses one who is homosexual.

Judith is a female version of a rather commonplace figure in contemporary literature, the sensitive and lonely hero of the *Bildungsroman*. She shares with that hero the characteristics of intense seriousness, lack of humor, egoism, and eventual disillusionment with the real world. Her consciousness is effectively revealed through Rosamond Lehmann's skillful use of the third-person point of view. Judith's growth is illuminated by the innumerable fragments of memories, conversations, sensual images, and reflections which make up her consciousness. But these are *not* presented in a similarly fragmented style. There is no attempt to capture her "stream of consciousness." Instead, the fragments are put into a logical and dramatic order by the intelligence of the third-person narrator. This technique of the limited point of view is particularly fitting for the study of a character who views the whole world—people and nature—self-reflexively. Judith is really the novel; other people are alive only because she thinks about them.

Such a technique is especially impressive in capturing the obsessive quality of her consciousness. She is depicted as a young woman who has been lonely all her life. An only child, educated by tutors, she has learned to use her intelligence—or, rather, her imagination—as a companion. Thus the fantasies she has created about other people are more satisfying than any real contact with them could be. Seen in this light, her obsession with Roddy appears reasonable. Since he is the most strange and aloof male who comes her way—the most opaque—her obsession with him is really an obsession with a fiction. Roddy is undefined as a character, especially so if one compares him with Martin or Julian, who are also viewed through Judith's perceptions but who emerge with greater precision. Roddy can be loved by Judith because he is part of herself; she creates him. Roddy's emotions are not deeply explored in the novel, only suggested. But since his incompleteness of character comes to us through Judith's eyes, it tells us a great deal about Judith. Since the novel is about *her* world and *her* reactions to it, her inability to make Roddy a complete human being gives us a clue to her failure in handling her relationship with him. Roddy is "shadowy" because Judith sees only the characteristics which are similar to her own—his loneliness, his lack of ease in the world, his romantic disgust with conventionality. If Judith had been able to view him differently, to explain him clearly, fully, to make him into a complete human being, the obsessiveness of her perception would have disappeared. But then we would have a different story. This one is *about* obsession and illusion. Although Judith's destruction of illusion leaves her empty, gives her a "dusty answer," it is a necessary and inevitable process that she must go through on her way to maturity. This she finally understands at the end of the novel:

> The old yearning to know, to understand, returned for a moment, and was followed by an utter blankness; and she knew that she had never known Roddy. He had never been for her. He had not once, for a single hour, become a part of real life. He had been a recurring dream, a figure seen always with abnormal clarity and complete distortion. The dream had obsessed her whole life with the problem of its significance, but now she was rid of it. [*Dusty Answer*, p. 346]

Judith's obsession with Roddy is balanced with another. When she goes to Cambridge she falls in love with a beautiful girl, Jennifer. Her two loves are oddly complementary; an undertone of homosexuality ties them together. The shadowy side of Roddy is a hint of a love affair between him and another man. That is what makes for his aloofness, frigidity, and eventually brutal treatment of Judith. It is as if Judith and Roddy are really separated from each other by their mutual inabilities to transcend the sense of "otherness" in each other. They are both pushed and motivated by the narcissistic obsessions growing out of their childhood. This androgynous strain emerging in *Dusty Answer* is again an indication of the changing relations between the sexes which so disturbs all the love affairs in these novels.

It is interesting to note that Judith's relationship with Jennifer follows a pattern similar to those of Miriam Henderson with Amabel and Clarissa Dalloway with Sally Seton. Three self-involved young women are attracted to three vivacious, bold, and outspoken ones.[21] There is an almost uncanny similarity between the central consciousnesses of the heroines and their objects of affection in these three novels. Jennifer, like Amabel and Sally, represents spontaneity. She is outspoken, friendly, and beautiful, the focus of attention for the whole group of girls of which Judith is a part. Judith is attracted by her radiance: "The suddenness, thought Judith—the sureness, the excitement!...glorious, glorious creature of warmth and colour! Her blue eyes had a wild brilliance between their thick lashes....Oh, Jennifer!" (p. 148).

Almost three pages are occupied with Judith's rapturous descriptions of her relationship with Jennifer: Jennifer entering a room, Jennifer singing folk songs, Jennifer chattering:

> Always Jennifer, It was impossible to drink up enough of her; and a day without her was a day with the light gone. [P. 148]

21. It might be noted here that Woolf's *Mrs. Dalloway* was published in 1925, *Dusty Answer* in 1927 (the same year as *To the Lighthouse*, which also has an androgynous aspect to it), and Dorothy Richardson's *Dawn's Left Hand* (which deals with Miriam's friendship with Amabel) in 1931. In the meantime, Radcliffe Hall's famous novel on lesbianism, *The Well of Loneliness*, appeared in 1928. Jeanette H. Foster in *Sex Variant Women in Literature* (London: Frederick Muller, 1958), p. 288, points out that *Dusty Answer* probably was the major literary influence on a whole group of novels, primarily by American writers, dealing with homosexuality in boarding schools and college dorms. Be that as it may, all these novels reflect a definite change in concepts of feminine consciousness and the acceptance of its portrayal in popular works of fiction.

Jennifer's boldness and defiance contrast greatly with Judith's introverted personality:

> Jennifer basking in popularity, drawing them all to her with a smile and a turn of the head, doing no work, breaking every rule, threatened with disgrace, plunged in despair; emerging the next moment new-bathed in radiance, oblivious of storm and stress. [P. 148]

Judith understands, in part, the narcissistic nature of the attraction, the need to complete herself through Jennifer.

> . . . She was the part of you which you never had been able to untie and set free, the part that wanted to dance and run and sing, taking strong draughts of wind and sunlight; and was, instead, done up in intricate knots and overcast with shadows; the part that longed to look outward and laugh, accepting life as an easy exciting thing; and yet was checked by a voice that said doubtfully that there were dark ideas behind it all, tangling the web; and turned you inward to grope among the roots of thought and feeling for the threads. [P. 155]

Like Clarissa and Miriam, the reflective, inhibited, doubting, questioning heroine compares herself with a freer woman. And, instead of envying her, she *loves* the woman who embodies those qualities lacking in herself.

But there is a major difference between Jennifer and her counterparts. Jennifer doesn't retreat into a submissive marriage at the end. In fact, unlike Amabel and Sally, Jennifer never shows any interest in men whatsoever. The reader may surmise that Jennifer's eventual direction will be homosexual, even if Judith might be unaware of that possibility. But Judith is aware of the basic differences between herself and Jennifer's new partner; she watches Jennifer and Geraldine wrestling on the lawn: ". . . because you were seeing that girl plainly, tall, dark and splendid, striding on the lawn with Jennifer, grasping her in strong arms, a match for her in all magnificent unfeminine physical ways, as you had never been" (p. 178).

When Judith tries to return to Jennifer at the end of the novel, she seems to be reaching back to the warmth and security she felt before she let herself be hurt by men. Her desire to escape from sexual relationships at this point reveals her disillusionment, her fatigue. And it also points up what will become a predominant theme in Rosamond Lehmann's novels: the inability of men and women to be successful with one another. Grace Fairfax in A Note in Music never escapes the unromantic, isolating relationship she has with her husband; her obsession with Hugh (who, like Roddy, appears to be homosexual) is futile. Rollo fails Olivia in The Weather in the Streets, returning to his wife and the safety of their life together. Finally, in The Echoing Grove (1953) the split between the sexes is complete. The two sisters, Madeleine and Dinah, are left alone together after their destructive pursuit of Rickie—married to Madeleine, lover of Dinah, torn apart by the conflict. The women, however, for all their unhappiness, emerge as the stronger sex. Dinah's explanation of the difficulties of women in the post–World War II years may be considered an explicit statement of the conflict which has run through all the novels:

> I can't help thinking it's particularly difficult to be a woman just at present. One feels so transitional and fluctuating...so I suppose do men. I believe we *are* all in flux—that the difference between our grandmothers and us is far deeper than we realize—much more fundamental than the obvious social economic one. Our so-called emancipation may be a symptom, not a cause. Sometimes I think it's more than the development of a new attitude towards sex: that a new [gender][22] may be evolving—psychically new—a sort of hybrid. Or else it's just beginning to be uncovered how much woman there is in man and *vice versa*. . . . Perhaps when we understand more, unearth more of what goes on in the unconscious, we shall manage to behave better to one another. It's ourselves we're trying to destroy when we're destructive: at least I think that explains the people who never can sustain a human relationship. It's not good and evil struggling in them: it's the suppressed unaccepted unacceptable man or women in them they have to cast out...can't come to terms with. [P. 363]

22. It is curious that in the American edition of The Echoing Grove the word "sex" appears in this spot rather than "gender," which is used in the British edition (London: Collins, 1953), p. 311. "Gender," of course, comes closer to the distinctions I pointed out in my introduction.

Five

Doris Lessing

NEAR the end of Rosamond Lehmann's last novel is an observation that the old sexual roles are dying out and a new "gender" emerging, an implicit recognition that what Dinah and Madeleine experienced in their relations with men are not merely isolated aberrations but symptoms of a much greater social—perhaps even biological—condition. It would appear that the individualistic conception of feminine consciousness which characterized the earlier novels in this study has been permanently altered by the mass destruction of World War II. One also senses this in Virginia Woolf's last novel. *Between the Acts* (1941), with its use of a violent sexual struggle between man and wife and its constant images of airplanes, fires in the distance, and rumors of bombings, indicates the intrusion of violence into her world. As in Rosamond Lehmann's *The Echoing Grove* (1953), the consciousnesses of the characters are pulled apart by the awareness of brutality. But these novels are the last ones for their authors, and serve mainly to demonstrate how the horror of war shocked and disrupted consciousnesses which were already formed.

The novels of Doris Lessing (1919–), however, shape the consciousness of women who never knew a world not marked by violence, hatred, and bigotry. Martha Quest may not have observed directly what Dinah (in *The Echoing Grove*) saw during the bombings of London, yet her experience of the war, even given the blurring effect of distance, exerts greater influence upon her still developing consciousness. Although Martha lives in an out-of-the-way, protected part of white-dominated Africa and experiences the war primarily through newsreels or stories of concentration camps told by escaped refugees, it, nonetheless, serves to symbolize more totally the permanent condition of the human race in the twentieth century.

With the global events of the time as an ever-present background, Doris Lessing's novels seem far removed from the individualistic focus of the earlier ones in this study. She is the only one to place the "feminine consciousness" within a political context. Martha Quest may be searching for reality in ways similar to Dorothy Richardson's Miriam Henderson, but Miriam, the "Tory anarchist" who develops her individualistic self in opposition to society, has been played out during the century. Doris Lessing connects each stage of Martha's development with external conditions like class conflict, racism, and war in order to make clear that she is primarily concerned with "a study of the individual conscience in its relations with the collective."[1] As a consequence, self-realization must of necessity be limited. The fate of any one woman is tied to the fate of women (and men) in general. Moreover, what is determined in human existence tends to make for a sameness in human beings. Thus Doris Lessing explained to Florence Howe during an interview, "I don't think we are as extraordinary as we like to think we are. We are more like other people than we would wish to believe. The same people occur again and again in our lives. Situations do. . . ."[2]

The repetitiveness of human experience and the basic powerlessness of individuals determined by their personal and cultural histories make the search for "freedom" difficult to achieve indeed. But for Doris Lessing's women that search is essential, some-

1. Doris Lessing, "The Small Personal Voice," in *Declaration*, ed. Tom Maschler (London: Macgibbon and Kee, 1957), p. 22.
2. Florence Howe, "A Conversation with Doris Lessing (1966)," *Contemporary Literature*, 14 (Autumn, 1973), 429.

thing they must do in order to achieve any degree of autonomy. Anna Wulf in *The Golden Notebook* (1962)[3] refers to herself and others like her as "boulder-pushers" (using an image reminiscent of Camus) in their attempts to break the cycle of destruction. It is a struggle that must be continuous, and one in which even monumental effort may, in the end, only result in the smallest push forward. This picture of human effort which emerges from Doris Lessing's novels continually suggests the smallness and weakness of individual human beings. Consequently, the whole subject of consciousness itself needs to be considered within this perspective. The cosmic view of humanity which emerges in *Briefing for a Descent into Hell* (1971)[4] complements the descriptions of Africa in the earlier novels, with their abundance of ants, locusts, and other insects. For even here the individual mind is "a pulse in a great darkness" (*The Golden Notebook*, p. 407), and the landscape of the mind itself resembles more the vastness and dryness of Africa than the water-soaked, protected isles of Great Britain. The usual metaphors for consciousness, streams and fountains,[5] may better be replaced by those of plains and vast spaces, and eventually even by the infinitude of space, of wavelengths, distances.

In *The Four-Gated City* (1969), the last novel of the *Children of Violence* series,[6] Martha Quest completes her search for reality by envisioning a new race of human beings whose minds have been expanded to fit them for life involved with distances; they have an extrasensory perception which enables them to "tune in" to a shared consciousness. It is at this point that one becomes aware of the difficulties inherent in containing this level of consciousness within the confines of the conventional novel. The

3. Doris Lessing, *The Golden Notebook* (New York: Simon & Schuster, 1962), p. 529.

4. Doris Lessing, *Briefing for a Descent into Hell* (New York: Alfred A. Knopf, 1971).

5. Anna uses the conventional image of the well and the source in her own novel within the novel (*The Golden Notebook*, pp. 336–37). Its ineffectiveness there might be a purposeful statement about its limitations as a metaphor.

6. Doris Lessing, *The Four-Gated City* (New York: Alfred A. Knopf, 1969). The other volumes in the series are: *Martha Quest*, 1952; *A Proper Marriage*, 1954; *A Ripple from the Storm*, 1958; *Landlocked*, 1965 (all reprinted, New York: Plume Books, 1970).

"stream of consciousness" was always an awkward metaphor in relation to Doris Lessing's work, and it is especially inadequate in this context, implying as it does an individual stream made up of personal associations separated from the "streams" of others. Perhaps Doris Lessing has used Anna Wulf's psychoanalysis with a Jungian analyst in *The Golden Notebook* as a tentative reference point along the way. What Jung called the "collective unconscious" might serve as the connection between Anna's own personal experiences and the universal significance of those experiences. Instead of a personal stream, there might be Jung's "ocean of images," accessible to everyone. Charles Watkins's preliminary mental journey over the world's oceans in *Briefing* might be a reflection of it. The difficulty, however, is in ordering this vastness, in joining the "individual" to the "collective" without making a work so esoteric (like Joyce's *Finnegans Wake*) that it cannot communicate to the uninitiated.[7] This is important, since for Doris Lessing the novel must also serve to teach, to be a social instrument (in fact, in her latest novels, to reveal and prophesy as well). *The Four-Gated City*, with its forecast of the destruction of Western civilization and its suggestion that individuals with the capacity for extrasensory perception are the evolutionary forerunners of a race of humans more fit for survival, points out the direction, but it better depicts the dissolution of individual consciousnesses and the society which is made up of them than it demonstrates the communal consciousness of the future.

Any definition of "feminine consciousness," then, in the novels of Doris Lessing must certainly take into account this inseparable connection between the individual and the race, and must also consider in this context the relevance of what is defined as "feminine" to the survival of the race. What becomes quickly apparent is the inappropriateness of so many "feminine" emotions and values to the larger crises of humanity itself.

The concern with evolutionary process which was hinted at in Rosamond Lehmann's *The Echoing Grove*, when Dinah remarked that "a new gender may be evolving—psychically new,"

7. See Anna's discussion with her analyst on why she does not "hold the aristocratic view of art" (*The Golden Notebook*, p. 406).

goes much further with Doris Lessing. And it is even clearer that her female characters are caught in the middle of an evolutionary stage where there is conflict between the old expectations for women and their dysfunction in the world they live in. Wherever one looks in Doris Lessing's fiction, at Martha Quest's awakening adolescence or Kate Brown's darkening womanhood in *The Summer before the Dark* (1973),[8] one finds a feminine consciousness in the process of disintegration.

Doris Lessing reveals this disintegration most fully through the consciousnesses of two characters: Martha Quest and Anna Wulf. Martha's consciousness is communicated to the reader as a part of the larger issue of the movement of twentieth-century history. Martha serves as a focus, as both a participant and an observer of the political, social, and cultural events of her times. Her consciousness is given to us not directly but through the device of a third-person omniscient narrator. Martha performs the function of the hero in a *Bildungsroman* throughout the *Children of Violence* series.[9] Hers is an evolving consciousness, and it is displayed at many stages as it grows. But the point of view is not that of someone looking back. This distinguishes Doris Lessing's treatment of Martha's consciousness from May Sinclair's organization of Mary Olivier's. Mary's story is told as a personal history; Mary looks back and selects details from the past which will enable the reader to understand the complete pattern which has already been put together. Martha's consciousness, on the other hand, is revealed gradually, without a sense of the pattern's being finished. In fact, the last volume, predicting the end of civilization and the destruction of all that contributed to Martha's consciousness, comes as a surprise, for even its style and organization seem of a different order than the earlier volumes. The shape of this series of novels is open-ended and haphazard, resembling the course of life itself.

Anna's consciousness, on the contrary, while seemingly disorganized and symptomatic of dissolution, is contained within a

8. Doris Lessing, *The Summer before the Dark* (New York: Alfred A. Knopf, 1973).

9. Doris Lessing calls *Children of Violence* a *Bildungsroman* in her notes at the end of *The Four-Gated City*, p. 615.

very rigid form. Within *The Golden Notebook* all possibilities are prearranged and structured; it is anything but open-ended. Doris Lessing has remarked that the point of *The Golden Notebook* is "the relation of its parts to each other."[10] "I understood that the shape of this book should be enclosed and claustrophobic —so narcissistic that the subject matter must break through the form."[11] But even though the form is narcissistic, and though it contains various approaches to Anna's mind, paradoxically it never gives us a direct view into her consciousness. All we know of Anna's consciousness is what she writes about it. And since a basic theme of the novel is the problem of defining reality in *words*—and the almost hopeless disparity between the complexity of reality and the simplicity of the abstractions used to contain it—Anna's *written* analysis of her consciousness must remain somewhat incomplete.

There are some important considerations here. First of all, it is only in the diaries (especially the blue one) that Anna expresses her own view of her consciousness. But this is Anna writing about her consciousness, not her consciousness itself. Writing necessarily involves a jump in time between the moment of consciousness of an experience and the moment of putting it down on paper. Writing is, therefore, an interpretation after the fact. Granted, Anna's ideas grow during the process of writing. But basically the journals contain Anna's memory of her consciousness. She has selected how she felt and what she saw and how she judges it. She is alone with her interpretation. This is what gives us that narcissistic effect. As a consequence, there is not the kind of penetration of consciousness that results from Dorothy Richardson's and Virginia Woolf's use of omniscient narrators to describe "objectively" what was going on in their characters' minds. They were able to express their characters' consciousnesses immediately, as they occurred in time, and not through memory. One must keep in mind

10. Doris Lessing, *Counterpoint*, ed. Ray Newquist (London: George All, 1965), p. 418.

11. Doris Lessing's remarks here come from the dust jacket of the first British edition. I have quoted them from Paul George Schleuter, "A Study of the Major Novels of Doris Lessing" (dissertation, Southern Illinois University, 1968), pp. 151–52.

also that even when Anna is described through a third-person point of view (in the "Free Women" sections), it is not her own consciousness which is communicated to us but, rather, Anna making herself a character in her own novel. It is again Anna reflecting upon Anna. Throughout the novel Anna is never given to us from another's point of view. And she is never shown in action, except as she describes herself in action when she fictionalizes herself.

Finally, the structure of *The Golden Notebook* resembles the condition of its main character's consciousness: fragmented. Anna's consciousness of herself is split up into several notebooks of different colors, and this separation symbolizes her relation to herself, to her body, to other people, and to society in general. Her own remark that "the novel has become a function of the fragmented society, the fragmented consciousness" (p. 59) corresponds with the structure of *The Golden Notebook* itself. Within it one finds a feminine consciousness suffering from alienation.

II   The evolution toward a universal consciousness in Doris Lessing's novels appears to begin with an approach to reality centered in the physical body and its relationship with nature. Even though Martha's rebellion starts initially on the basis of abstract ideas, yet it is surely through her body—as she later experiences sexual relationships, pregnancy, and childbirth—that her most profound discoveries are achieved. Eventually, at the very end of her "quest," she resembles several other women in this study in that she searches only with her mind—which has achieved new and special powers. Miriam Henderson's "pilgrimage" depended to a much greater degree on the faculty of vision—of perceiving through the eyes—which makes of reality a subjective phenomenon. Miriam's "knowing" through her body was limited, and she preferred to escape from it at the end into spiritual knowing. But knowing through the body makes up a large part of Martha's investigation of life (and of Anna Wulf's as well). Carnal knowledge, however, brings one away from the particularities of consciousness related only to the individual and into a "knowing" that is approachable for every human being. When Martha fears being dissolved during sex, she also is afraid of reaching that level in herself which she shares with all living creatures. Doris Lessing may be using the power of sexuality here to provide the dramatic physical manifestations of unity, but it is only one of the steps in her movement toward a recognition of the mental unity that is most fully revealed through the consciousness of Charles Watkins in *Briefing*. Another step is the analysis of dreams—of the archetypes symbolized by images pulled up from the collective unconscious that we experience through Anna Wulf's psychoanalysis in *The Golden Notebook*. But Martha will go even further. At the end she recognizes a truly diffused consciousness, in which through the proper training and innate predisposition (note the implied determinism here), one consciousness may actually "tune in" to another. At the last, then, the boundaries of individual thought patterns (symbolized so often in twentieth-century literature by those carefully delineated riverbeds) are illusions.

This is where it all ends; Martha's quest will finally take her out of her body. But it begins inside it, and those first uncertain questionings of the way society has taught her to consider her physicality form the beginning of the basic conflict in her feminine consciousness. The young Martha is still caught up in her need to identify herself as a separate ego; her disassociation of mind and body then typifies the alienated condition of modern life. The following is a good example:

> During this rite, she remained passive, offering herself to his adoration; she was quite excluded; she was conscious of every line and curve of her own body, as if she were scrutinizing it with his eyes. And for hours, or so it seemed, he kissed and adored, pressing his body humbly against her and withdrawing it, and she waited for him to sate his visual passion and allow her to forget the weight of her limbs, her body, felt as something heavy and white and cold, separate from herself. [*Martha Quest*, p. 220]

This disassociation (and the accompanying objectification of the body itself) complements the increasing objectification of people which takes place as the violence of modern life increases. Martha gets angry when Douglas refers to her breasts as "*Them*—just as if they had nothing to do with me!" (*Martha Quest*, p. 220). She begins to realize that not only do men separate a woman's body from her mind, but they tend to view her body as a collection of separate pieces as well, evidenced by their idolization of parts of the body: breasts, legs, etc. This fragmentation of body is but another example of the division and fragmentation of mind which mark the modern consciousness.

Accordingly Martha and her first husband, Douglas, turn to books (sex manuals, psychology texts) for guidance, which only increases her real belief that the body is something that has a value of its own, separate from her as a person. It must be "handled" and "used" properly:

> . . . It was almost with the feeling of a rider who was wondering whether his horse would make the course that she regarded this body of hers, which was not only divided from her brain by the necessity of keeping open that cool and dispassionate eye, but separated into compartments of its own. Martha had after all been provided with a map of her flesh by "the book," in which each area was marked by the name of a different physical sensation, so that her mind was anxiously aware, not only of a disconnected partner, a body, but of every part of it, which might or might not come up to scratch at any given occasion. There were moments when she felt she was strenuously held together by nothing more than an act of will. She was beginning to feel that this view of herself was an offense against what was deepest and most real in her. And again she thought of the simple women of the country, who might be women in peace, according to their instincts, without being made to think and disintegrate themselves into fragments. [*A Proper Marriage*, p. 63]

Yet Martha is so afraid of losing herself that the very completeness of mind and body which she associates with the country women would terrify her if she were able to experience it. Later, when she falls in love for the first time (after she has been married twice), she resists her feelings at first because of this fear of losing herself: "No, it was too strong . . . much easier to live deprived . . . *to be self-contained*. No, she did not want to be dissolved" (*Landlocked*, p. 99).

The ego that is self-contained, however, is only a whole because of the exclusion of whatever will reveal its nature. For it is not a unity at all but a combination of fragments. To let herself be carried away on the tide of primal drives, joining her with the forces of nature—these might make her realize that reality itself is chaos. But much later, in *The Four-Gated City*, Martha understands that the very dissolution through sexuality she once feared is only a dissolution of what is, in reality, already in fragments. On the contrary, then, what seems like dissolution during complete sexual experience works paradoxically as a bringing together, a unifying function:

> . . . She had never really seen before how the separate parts of herself went on, working individually by themselves, not joining: that was the condition of being "normal" as we understand it. Breath flows on, blood beats on, separately from each other; my sex lives on there, responding or not; my heart feels this and that, and my mind up here goes working on, quite different from the heart; yet when the real high place of sex is reached, everything moves together, it is just that moment when everything does move together that makes the gears shift up. Yet people regarded sex as the drainer, the emptier, instead of the maker of energy. [*The Four-Gated City*, p. 61]

Although Martha finally becomes able to be drawn into an encounter with these greater forces, it is interesting to find that she must still objectify other human beings in order to do so. She becomes conscious that it has "nothing to do with Jack the person, he's the instrument that knows how to reach it" (*The Four-Gated City*, p. 59). The word "instrument" is illuminating because it, like so many other terms in this last novel of the series, is part of an imagery of electronic technology. In fact, objectification has now gone so far that individuals may actually consider other people "instruments" to help them "tune in" to different wavelengths of experience. Thus the imagery of sex moves out of the mechanical (an earlier, and simpler, form of objectification) into the electronic—and finally to the telepathic. The lovers "came to themselves light and easy, and as if they had been washed through and through by currents of energy. She felt as if she had been connected to a dynamo, the centre of her life" (p. 61). Much later in the novel, when Martha becomes aware of her own extrasensory powers, she realizes that an interchangeability between one person and another is possible in sex as well as through minds alone. She speaks of the energy two lovers make, "like conductors of conduits for the force which moved them" (p. 470). And she is made aware of "an impersonal current which she brought from Mark, who had it from Lynda, who had it from...the impersonal sea" (p. 471). "Impersonal," of course, is the essential word. And it defines, at the last, the relationship of human being to human being, and human being to nature: "Great forces as impersonal as thunder or lightning or sunlight or the movement of the oceans being contracted and heaped and rolled in their beds by the moon, swept through bodies, and now she knew quite well why Mark had come blindly upstairs to the nearest friendly body, being in the grip of this force—or *a* force, one of them. Not sex. Not necessarily. Not unless one chose to make it so" (pp. 470–71).

Martha was conscious of "great forces as impersonal as thunder" long before she understood their connection with sexuality, however. Her first intimations of their connections with her own body took place during her pregnancy and then while giving birth to her daughter, Caroline. With Doris Lessing, as with Rosamond Lehmann, pregnancy is used to demonstrate the struggle between individual will and the forces of nature; it is a struggle in which a woman loses control over her own body in a way more dramatic than any other (even more than aging, because that takes so long that consciousness almost has time to take it in; pregnancy is an abrupt affront to the ego). Its first insult is the change it effects on her body:

> The skin on the lower slopes was breaking into purple weals; on the upper part of the thighs were red straining patches. Her breasts were heavy, bruised-looking. But the woman who only a few months before had enjoyed such ecstasies of self-worship had apparently died. She felt no more than a pang for the lost perfection.... She reminded herself that she would never be perfect again. . . . It was gone, that brief flowering. [*A Proper Marriage*, p. 136]

Martha's changing consciousness during pregnancy resembles that of Olivia in Rosamond Lehmann's *The Weather in the*

Streets. Like Olivia, she becomes increasingly involved in her own body and the sensations within it. She moves more totally into herself as the pregnancy progresses. Her perceptions of time alter; she might discover that her husband has left in the morning and returned from work to find her still sitting in the same place: "To her it was as if vast stretches of time had passed. Inside her stomach the human race had fought and raised its way through another million years of its history; that other time was claiming her . . . it was becoming an effort to recognize the existence of anything outside this great central drama" (p. 113).

Martha's response to her pregnancy corresponds with her general philosophic stance of rebellion against the concept of necessity. Continually she struggles to assert her individuality against the demands of her body, which now is alien, allied with all those determining powers of family, society, and nature:

> She was essentially divided. One part of herself was sunk in the development of the creature, appallingly slow, frighteningly inevitable, a process which . . . dragged her back into the impersonal blind urges of creation; with the other part she watched it; her mind was like a lighthouse, anxious and watchful that she, the free spirit, should not be implicated; and engaged in daydreams of the exciting activities that could begin when she was liberated. [P. 121]

The struggle continues and reaches its climax during Martha's labor and delivery. The dislocation of the "normal" sequences of perception affects her as remarkable, puzzling. The whole notion of ordinary "time" breaks up in her consciousness:

> Martha noted that something new was happening to time. The watch that lay six inches from her nose on her crooked arm said the pains were punctual at two minutes. But from the moment that the warning hot wave of pain swept up her back, she entered a place where there was no time at all. An agony so unbelievable gripped her that her astounded and protesting mind cried out it was impossible such pain should be. It was a pain so violent that it was no longer pain, but a condition of being. Every particle of flesh shrieked out, while the wave spurted like an electric current from somewhere in her backbone and through her in shock after shock. [P. 144]

But the pain ends, and the condition of painlessness between contractions is as total as the intensity of the pain. She cannot "remember" the pain when it is over, neither can she remember the painlessness in the midst of the pain: "They were two states of being, utterly disconnected, without a bridge, and Martha found herself in a condition of anxious but exasperated anger that she could *not* remember the agony fifteen seconds after it had ended" (p. 144). Instead, she becomes absorbed in her own anger at her inability to connect the two parts of herself. She cannot even "imagine" the pain or the no-pain: "With all her determination, she could not. There were two Marthas, and there was nothing to bridge them. Failure. Complete failure. She was helpless with rage" (p. 145).

III   Decades earlier May Sinclair referred to woman as "the sex that pays," and this theme certainly underlies the attitudes of Doris Lessing's women no less than Rosamond Lehmann's or May Sinclair's. But the form of its exposition has changed. The physical details associated with the "suffering" are elaborated, made clinical; the whole process of childbirth is explained in full, giving it a "modern" frankness. Yet the attitude of Martha toward what is happening to her does not differ greatly from that of her predecessors. The one difference that stands out is her awareness of a historical perspective—an awareness that her own personal history (and the history of her culture) has conditioned her response. When Martha first thinks about it, it is in relation to her friend Alice's pregnancy; she does not consciously know yet that she is also pregnant:

> Her emotions were violent and mixed. She felt towards the pregnant woman, the abstraction, a strong repulsion which caused various images, all unpleasant, to rise into her mind one after another. From her childhood came a memory of lowered voices, distasteful intimacies, hidden sicknesses. . . . Alice, because she was pregnant, was delivered back into the hands of the old people. . . . She felt caged, for Alice. She could feel the bonds around herself. She consciously shook them off and exulted in the thought that she was free. Free! . . . But at the same time a deeper emotion

was turning towards Alice, with an unconscious curiosity, warm, tender, protective. It was an emotion not far from envy. . . . But no sooner had she put it into words than she reacted back again with a shuddering impulse towards escape. She could see the scene: Alice, loose and misshapen, with an ugly wet-mouthed infant, feeding-bottles, napkins, smells. [*A Proper Marriage*, p. 91]

Part of Martha's revulsion at the idea of motherhood stems from the negative cultural attitudes toward it which were instilled in her during childhood, but the other part of her distaste is associated with her belief that history repeats itself, that it runs in cycles, and that she may not escape the influences from the past but will perpetuate them if she bears a child. It is within this context that the whole subject of determinism becomes most obvious. The key word in the passage quoted above is "free," repeated to intensify its meaning. "Free" is in opposition to pregnant. And when Martha studies her own mother, she sees herself in her mother's place, each of them without "any validity as persons, but . . . mere pawns in the hands of an old fatality" (p. 94). She sees themselves as part of a long series of mothers and daughters, irrevocably linked with "a series of shadowy dependent men, broken-willed and sick with compelled diseases" (p. 94).

Martha's knowledge of the collapse of bourgeois society and its reflection in the destructive patterns of modern family life comes through reading the popularizers of nineteenth-century deterministic thinkers, reflecting many of the same notions that troubled Mary Olivier: ". . . This the nightmare, this the nightmare of a class and generation: repetition. And although Martha had read nothing of the great interpreters of the nightmare, she had been soaked in the minor literature of the last thirty years, which had dealt with very little else: a series of doomed individuals, carrying their doom *inside* them, like the seeds of a fatal disease" (p. 95). But added to these is a new influence, and a most crucial one: Marxism. Martha's slim hope of breaking the deterministic chain is through some sort of radical action; she feels that it is "in her power to cut the cycle" by refusing to bear children. Yet Martha is already pregnant when she makes this decision.

Martha later tries to escape again by leaving her husband and child: wishing "freedom" for her child through the act of leaving her. Nonetheless, in *The Four-Gated City* Martha feels that her rebellion against the determinism of the family was futile. She explains bitterly to Jack how she left her little girl, how she believed that Communism had the answer:

> "Oh, sometimes I think Communism, for people who weren't in Communist countries, it was a kind of litmus paper, a hold-all—you took from it what you wanted. But for us it went without saying that the family was a dreadful tyranny, a doomed institution, a kind of a mechanism for destroying everyone. . . . And so we abolished the family. . . . And then there would be the golden age, no family, no neurosis. Because the family was the source of neurosis. The father would be a stud and the mother an incubator, and the children handed at birth to an institution: for their own good, you understand, to save them from the inevitability of their corruption. . . . Do you know how many people have become Communists simply because of that: because Communism would do away with the family? But Communism has done no such thing, it's done the opposite." [Pp. 66–67]

May Sinclair had Mary Olivier fighting the determinism of heredity and environment manifested in her family, but not extending it to the society as a whole, especially to the economic determinism which Marxist theory connects with the others. Mary's rebellion—if one compares it with Martha's hostility—seems remarkably polite. Martha's revolt is full of the fury of self-hate fueled by an understanding that she reflects what is wrong with her family, and her family what is wrong with society in general (and here her awareness of the injustices of racism, economic exploitation, violence, add weight to her argument). Thus she tries to cut out what there is of her family in herself, and dreams of a golden age—"the four-gated city" of peace and community—that is in direct opposition to what her family represents. Martha hates her mother so intensely because of her own horror that she might become like her. For what is always a consideration in her mind is that there just might not be anything in her *besides* what she has been given. Years after Martha breaks from her family, her mother returns to haunt her by visiting England. This visit drives Martha to the point of madness. She cannot accept her mother—more to the point, she cannot accept that part of herself which *is* her mother. The concept of heredity has so burned itself into her consciousness that even during sexual intercourse she finds it filtering into her mind as a consideration in her sense of self-identity: "Her face which was,—whose? For her eyes were her father's, and her mouth too; and her nose and the shape of her face and even where the lines showed how they would fall, and a mole, her mother's. Yet it was Martha who lay now, endowed with those features which were not hers at all, merely from stock, the storehouse of the race" (*The Four-Gated City*, p. 57).

If biology plays a predominant part in Doris Lessing's women's consciousness of determinism, the other part is their role in society. Florence Howe has pointed out the irony in the words "Free Women," which form the title of Anna Wulf's own novel in *The Golden Notebook*. For although they are free to work and to raise children alone, they are still bound to their female functions by biology and by culture.[12] Indeed, nowhere is the conflict between freedom and restraint clearer than in these women's attitudes toward their children and their maternal role. Anna remarks that "having a baby is where women feel they are entering into some sort of inevitable destiny" (*The Golden Notebook*, p. 532). The role of mother is an enactment of that destiny, a continual responsibility that alters the consciousness of these women. Martha Quest becomes a mother against her wishes, then feels pulled along by a role she has not united with her concept of herself. She is resentful of the intrusions into her mobility. She cannot accept living her life "regulated by the clock of Caroline's needs" (*A Proper Marriage*, p. 201). Her consciousness at this point is rigid with conflict:

12. "As heterosexual women, they are sexually dependent on men. They are also bound by biological as well as cultural drives to child-bearing and motherhood. Hence, the 'free' woman is free only in a most limited sense. She is free to choose between her divided selves: free to attempt the 'precarious balance' of living with both of them; free to be 'female' or to be a 'free woman.' Finally, free comes to mean divided. The free woman divided in Mrs. Lessing's novels, suffers most from a feeling of failure" (Florence Howe, "Doris Lessing's Free Women," *Nation*, 200 (Jan. 11, 1965), 34).

. . . She wished it were already the end of the day, and Caroline
safely in bed and asleep. Then her, Martha's life might begin.
And yet the hours of evening were as restless and dissatisfied; she
always went to bed early to put an end to them. Her whole life
was a hurrying onwards, to get it past; she was back in the tension
of hurry, hurry, hurry; and yet there was nothing at the end of it
to hurry towards, not even the end of the war, which would
change nothing for her.

At this point in her reflections, she again told herself to relax:
her inability to enjoy Caroline simply filled her with guilt. Yet
she could not relax into Caroline; that would be a disloyalty and
even a danger to herself. Cycles of guilt and defiance ruled her
living and she knew it; she had not the beginnings of an understanding what it all meant. [P. 201]

Martha is alone with her baby during this section of the novel:
Douglas is in the army. The consideration of motherhood here,
as in *The Golden Notebook*, revolves around the notion of an
isolated relationship between mother and child. Missing are the
complex associations of mother, father, and other children. Of
course, that complexity makes the role of mother even more
consuming (witness Mrs. Ramsay's need for moments of solitude
in *To the Lighthouse*). But when Doris Lessing's women experience it as women without husbands, she links the role more directly with another social concern; for "free women," women
alone, divorced, families split up, are not unusual phenomena in
modern society. And the increased emotional burden on the woman who must do it all alone may underscore what is *basic* to the
role—the loss of a woman's daily freedom. Anna Wulf writes
about "the control and discipline of being a mother" (*The Golden Notebook*, p. 286) that she must maintain in order to fulfill
all the demands of her day. When her daughter Janet is old
enough to go away to school, Anna remarks on her own new sense
of herself as a separate entity: "I haven't moved, at ease, in time,
since Janet was born. Having a child means being conscious of
the clock, never being free of something that has to be done at a
certain moment ahead. An Anna is coming to life that died when
Janet was born" (p. 468).

Doris Lessing takes the effects of motherhood much further

with Kate Brown in *The Summer before the Dark*. Kate, wife of a successful physician, mother of four grown children, looks back at her years as a housewife and sees how "an unafraid young creature had been turned, through the long, grinding process of always, always being at other people's beck and call, always having to give out attention to detail, minuscule wants, demands, needs, events, crises, into an obsessed maniac" (p. 105).

IV   Rebellion, acquiescence, rebellion, acquiescence—they reappear in continual cycles within Doris Lessing's women's consciousnesses. The rebellion stands out boldly: rage against the family, the system, the oppression of human beings. But the submission, the passivity, which lies so close behind the other seems —ironically perhaps—the more dominant characteristic of consciousness. In the case of Martha Quest, who finds herself married twice to men she does not love, who bears a child after she decided she would not, who winds up in the Coldridge household permanently as caretaker and helpmeet, sailing along from one situation to the next with plans for change, plans for decisive action, but nonetheless carried along on a tide of contingency—for that Martha passivity almost approaches tropism. Things just seem to happen to Martha. And what happens goes against the direction of her thoughts. As Walter Allen put it, "She seems at times, to drift in an almost somnambulistic state, caught as she is between the pressure to conform (not only to the local mores but also, as it were, biologically, as a woman), and the urge, intermittent but increasingly insistent, to be free to make her own life."[13] Early in the series she is described as "submitting herself to a person or a place, with a demure, childish compliance, as if she were under a spell . . . she did not consciously expect or demand; she might dream about things being different, but that, after all, commits one to nothing" (*Martha Quest*, p. 149). Accordingly, before her first marriage she feels "she could not help it; she was being dragged towards it, whether she liked it or not" (*Martha Quest*, p. 243).

13. Walton Allen, "Martha the Rebel," *New York Times Book Review* (Nov. 15, 1964), p. 52.

Martha's actions (and some of them are quite dramatic and irrevocable, such as deciding to leave her child) are yet accompanied by the most passive yearnings. She is often in a state of waiting, waiting for a man to create a "self" for her:

> There is a type of woman who can never be, as they are likely to put it, "themselves" with anyone but the man to whom they have permanently or not given their hearts. If the man goes away there is left an empty space filled with shadows. She mourns for the temporarily extinct person she can only be with a man she loves; she mourns him who brought her "self" to life. She lives with the empty space at her side, peopled with the images of her own potentialities until the next man walks into the space, absorbs the shadows into himself, creating her, allowing her to be her "self"—but a new self, since it is his conception which forms her. [A *Ripple from the Storm*, p. 38]

Since Martha's passivity is revealed more often by her behavior —which is often at odds with her attitudes—her consciousness does not always reflect it. Her thoughts are usually defiant and iconoclastic. But Anna Wulf's passivity is approachable *through* her consciousness. It is, moreover, elaborately considered in many forms as she tries to understand that part of herself. It comes out in her self-analyses, in her journals, and as she fictionalizes herself in novels and half-created stories. These fictions, which are the product of the *active* side of her consciousness since they result from her shaping and ordering of experience, might also be thought of as the attempt of her *active* self to understand her *passive* self. The yellow notebook probably provides the best source for interpreting Anna's problem with passivity.

Quite a few of the undeveloped story ideas Anna jots down in this notebook deal with submissiveness. For example, #8 is about a woman artist who uses her own talent to make an artist out of her lover, "as if she were a dynamo that fed energy into him" (*The Golden Notebook*, p. 458). Her identity is thus consumed by the male. Or in #18 a woman continually changes "in response to one man who is a psychological chameleon" (p. 461). Expressed obliquely through these hurried notations is Anna's fear that her own identity is undermined by men through her own lack of ego strength. But the most illuminating revelation of her problem may be found in the relationship between Anna and Ella, the heroine of her partially composed novel in the yellow notebook. They share many qualities, either directly or in the reverse (the same experiences with the names changed, or slightly altered, or totally opposite). Anna begins to form Ella's consciousness with elements from her own, but as she goes on she finds herself putting things into Ella that she only partially understands; or they may even be completely unconscious. Anna comments, "I don't understand what happens at the moment Ella separates herself from me and becomes Ella" (p. 393). Ella takes on a life of her own as she develops in Anna's novel, exemplifying in part the unconscious component of the creative act. When Ella goes out on her own, leaving her creator behind, she becomes the symbol of that creator's passivity.

As Ella emerges, she is revealed as tending more toward the conventional and the general than Anna. She is both more passive than the Anna of the blue notebook and more stereotyped. Her utterances echo sentiments from a popularized version of the psychology of sex that often sound just like the writing in the women's magazine Ella works for. The style of the yellow notebook is thus much cruder—and more incomplete—than in the others. Some parody is obviously intended (as in the embarrassing description of Ella's love-making with the "typical" American). However, it might also suggest Anna's attempt to communicate her ideas here in a "popular" form. Ella's consciousness, then, might correspond with a generalized statement of feminine consciousness by her creator, Anna. Through Ella, Anna may simplify and express the "typical" for a woman of her kind.

Thus Anna allows Ella to express a type of commonplace submissiveness. She shows her giving up all social life in order to be available to Paul (a situation very similar, by the way, to Olivia's in Rosamond Lehmann's *The Weather in the Streets*, where Olivia gives up all of hers in order to continue a secret affair with Rollo). Furthermore, Ella keeps up a fantasy about Paul's wife and even visits his house in her absence (Olivia did this also). Both Ella and Olivia imagine that their lovers' wives are conventional women, even though they never know them, while they think of themselves as rebels against conformity.

Ella is allowed to state (or think) the hackneyed phrases which may sum up the average "truth" but would, nevertheless, embarrass Anna if she used them about herself. Thus Anna describes Ella making love with Paul for the first time with: "But soon she gave herself up, and in confidence, because their bodies understood each other. (But it was only later, she would use a phrase like 'our bodies understood each other.' At the time, she was thinking: *We* understand each other)" (p. 168). Anna's first thought is to refer to Ella's experience with the words "their bodies understood each other," but that phrase stands out as a cliché so obvious it might as well have come straight from *True Confessions*. So Anna modifies it by drawing attention to it in her parenthetical comment. She reworks it, sophisticates it in a sense, so that the cliché operates on many levels. It is first of all a commentary on the stage Ella has reached in experience and understanding. And it is a symptom of Anna's own inability to "name" (reflected in her "writer's block") and her consciousness of that inability. Finally, it reveals Anna's attempt to rise above her limitations by altering the cliché—by putting it squarely within *Ella's* consciousness, escaping from the responsibility of it, so to speak.

Another use for Ella is as the recipient of statement. Much of the complexity of the ideas in the other notebooks comes through the richness of description, imagery, and extended narrative. But the single-mindedness and oversimplification of Anna's initial attempts at fictionalizing are revealed through her frequent use of statement to carry the burden of meaning. For instance, much of the discussion in the yellow notebook on the mechanics of sex comes about as Anna theorizes about Ella's (and her own) sexual responses. She discovers "that until I sat down to write about it, I had never analyzed how sex was between myself and Michael" (p. 186). What then follows is a long passage in which Anna tries to describe and analyze Ella's understanding of the difference between vaginal and clitoral orgasms. In it she works out the implied contrast between scientific (defined by inference as masculine) ways of looking at sex (Paul's statement that physiologists

don't find a physical basis for vaginal orgasm), and Ella's "feminine" reaction: "Then they don't know much, do they?" (p. 186).

Anna can only talk about the orgasm; she is unable to come up
with a new or illuminating image with which to contain it:

> The vaginal orgasm is a dissolving in a vague, dark generalized
> sensation like being swirled in a warm whirlpool. There are sev-
> eral different sorts of clitoral orgasms, and they are more powerful
> (that is a male word) than the vaginal orgasm. There can be a
> thousand thrills, sensations, etc., but there is only one real female
> orgasm and that is when a man, from the whole of his need and
> desire takes a woman and wants all her response. Everything else
> is a substitute and a fake, and the most inexperienced woman
> feels this instinctively. [P. 186]

Notice the pedantic, almost defensive tone of Anna's writing here.
The image is nearly lost in the explanation. But it serves to illustrate the essentially passive nature of the "real" orgasm. Anna
describes the vaginal orgasm as a *reaction* to the man. The man's
need comes first; the woman *responds* to that need. The man
then initiates, acts, performs; the woman is "swirled into a warm
whirlpool." The experience comes to the woman; she is drawn
into the whirlpool. Her will is not involved. Her body makes the
decision for her. Freudian precedents for this image and the explanation of it are not too far away. Anna's is an interpretation
of the sexuality of women that is as traditional by midcentury as
was Dorothy Richardson's interpretation of feminine thinking
during her time.[14]

Incidentally, Anna appears to accept a phrase like "when a man
... takes a woman" or the assumption that "powerful" is a "male
word" without question. She also seems to accept (if subconsciously, as it is stated through her fictionalization, Ella) a view of the
sexual attitudes of men and women which is equally traditional.
Later, when Ella considers going to bed with another man, she
realizes she cannot grant herself the same kind of emotional
freedom she thinks belongs to men: "Only yesterday I decided it
was ridiculous, women like me, having emotions that don't fit our

14. See Kate Millett's attack on the Freudian interpretation of women's sexuality in *Sexual Politics* (Garden City, N.Y.: Doubleday, 1970), pp. 176–203.

lives. A man now, in this situation, *the sort of man I would be if I'd been born a man,* would go to bed and think no more of it" (p. 276).

Much of the concern with sexuality expressed throughout the notebooks is based on very conventional notions of women's supposed sexual passivity. Thus in the blue notebook Anna writes about how she needs to help a man, to make him strong, so that finally she can be taken care of—that is, to become strong, *acting* in the interests of an ultimate passivity:

> I am always amazed, in myself and in other women at the strength of our need to bolster men up. This is ironical, living as we do in a time of men's criticizing us for being "castrating," etc.,—all the other words and phrases of the same kind. . . . For the truth is, women have this deep instinctive need to build a man up as a man. . . . I suppose this is because real men become fewer and fewer, and we are frightened, trying to create men.
>
> No, what terrifies me is my willingness. It is what Mother Sugar would call "the negative side" of the women's need to placate, to submit. Now I am not Anna, I have no will, I can't move out of a situation once it has started, I just go along with it. [P. 414]

Anna brings her uneasiness over her own lack of will directly into her consciousness at this point. She is frightened when she sees herself continuing a hopeless relationship with a man whose sexual problems prevent him from giving to a woman (or conversely). But she feels compelled to build him up even though her compulsion to do so works against her own best interests. Throughout the novel Anna and the other women are troubled over the disappearance of "real men." What this means is left vague, but there are few men in the novel who would qualify. They display a variety of sexual problems: impotence, premature ejaculation, homosexuality, sadism, and the inability to respond emotionally. The self-centeredness of most men in the novel illustrates their inability to commit themselves lovingly and completely to one woman; their hostility toward women is symptomatic of the outmoded character of traditional roles.

Anna's fear of her own lack of will is also related to her "writer's block"—her inability to *act* through writing any longer. She again uses Ella as the mouthpiece for her statement of the dilemma. She has Ella consider that she does not really care if she writes or not. Ella expects writing will come about on its own through "a kind of open readiness, a passive waiting. Then perhaps one day I'll find myself writing" (p. 269). Anna allows Ella to express her own hope that the writing block will resolve itself. "Passive waiting" is the key phrase (and one might notice how similar it is to Rosamond Lehmann's "the right kind of passivity"). But Ella's predicament lies in the fact that she does not really value her production, that is, the doing, the activity which writing represents, as much as she values the *being*, the passive state of being loved: "Suppose Paul had said to me, I'll marry you if you promise never to write another word? My God, I would have done it!" (p. 269). Ella counterpoises the notion of freedom with the reality of her emotions, and comes up with a statement about the differences between the emotions of men and women which is the same one made years ago by Miriam Henderson in Dorothy Richardson's *Pilgrimage*. When she points out that men prefer work and women prefer people, the statement has hardly changed its shape at all:[15]

> What is terrible is that after every one of the phases of my life is finished, I am left with no more than some banal commonplace that everyone knows: in this case, that women's emotions are all still fitted for a kind of society that no longer exists. My deep emotions, my real ones, are to do with my relationship with a man. One man. But I don't live that kind of life, and I know few women who do. So what I feel is irrelevant and silly . . . I am always coming to the conclusion that my real emotions are foolish, I am always having, as it were, to cancel myself out. I ought to be like a man, caring more for my work than for people; I ought to put my work first, and take men as they come, or find an ordinary comfortable man for bread and butter reasons—but I won't do it, I can't be like that.... [P. 269]

15. Ella also makes the following reflection: ". . . she thinks for the hundredth time that in their emotional life all these intelligent men use a level so much lower than anything they use for work, that they might be different creatures" (*The Golden Notebook*, p. 392).

The issue of passivity links both the attitudes about sex and creativity in the consciousnesses of these women. In a sense one might say that the ordering of consciousness in *The Golden Notebook* grows out of the passivity of its main character. Anna, letting her ideas fall where they may in whichever notebook seems best to fit her mood, refusing to write a conventional, publishable novel because she knows it cannot express her overwhelmed sensibility, gradually discovers that the fragmentation inherent in her decision to write in separate notebooks is also falsifying the truth. Thus she finally tries to bring everything together into one, "golden" notebook. If the organization of *The Golden Notebook* as a whole (that is, the overall arrangement of the parts) seems artificial, it still does appear that Doris Lessing has structured the novel this way in order to make it resemble the process of creativity. Through its many styles and forms it works from the unknown or half-known into the fictionalized "statement" (which is still tentative), and the reader goes along with the same process that Anna goes through as she continually comes to new insights which grow out of her observations and reflections. She grasps intermediate truths about herself, then slowly sees those truths in relation to the whole—which in its splitting apart is the magnifying-glass image of her own consciousness. The side of Anna which is torn between old values and new realities, between the belief in doing and the reality of *being done to*, which expresses the unconscious, helpless, passive woman as object (and women are viewed as objects in this society), corresponds with the shape of the novel as a whole. In contrast, the limitations in the ordering of the conventional novel are made abundantly clear by the inclusion of Anna's own "Free Women." Anna's attempt at a novel does not even hint at the truth. It is a failure. But *The Golden Notebook*, which admits of that failure of the limited order, is not. In it, "reality" or "truth" is never made absolute, for one is never certain where the truth is, let alone who is really giving the ultimate answer. Is it Ella? Anna? the persona of what story? what notebook?

V   Throughout this study the notion of feminine passivity has appeared and reappeared, and accordingly, so has that of feminine intuition. It is certainly not surprising, therefore, to find that the latter is as much a part of the consciousness of Doris Lessing's "free women" as it was with that early model of independence, Miriam Henderson. And as it was with Miriam, the interpretation of a feminine apperception of reality is troubled by the contradiction between the necessary use of abstractions—logical and sequential—in *writing* about reality, and the underlying belief in a spontaneous penetration to a reality which cannot be contained within the limits of abstraction. Although Martha and Anna may accept essentially rational explanations for behavior (either social and thus Marxist, or psychological and Jungian), at various stages in their development they strain at the limits of these explanations and finally go beyond them. Martha Quest's rebellion begins with concepts derived from books, from predominantly male thinkers. But her use of their ideas is an artificial defense; she uses them mechanically since she has not yet found a way of understanding life which grows out of her own mode of consciousness:

> She was engaged in examining and repairing those intellectual's bastions of defense behind which she sheltered that building whose shape had first been sketched so far back in her childhood she could no longer remember how it then looked . . . it was as if she, Martha, were a variety of soft, shell-less creature whose survival lay in the strength of those walls. Reaching out in all directions from behind it, she clutched at the bricks of arguments, the stones of words, discarding any that might not fit into the building. [*A Proper Marriage*, p. 94]

Martha protects herself with hard words. The imagery of intellect is all inanimate and solid, lifeless and rigid, inferring the dogmatism of her stance. Yet Martha herself is described as a "soft, shell-less creature," making her open and *receptive* by nature, even if she is overwhelmed by the chaos that openness must take in.

Martha's more basic reaction to abstractions is to distrust them. Although she has built the foundation of her revolt upon them, the direction of her psychic development is toward their rejection. By the time of *The Four-Gated City*, she has concluded that words, labels which people use to contain reality, actually stop the thinking process because they "sterilise," "partition off," or "compartmentalise" reality (p. 430).[16]

Anna Wulf's sense of self-identity has always been intimately related to the power of words. Since she is a writer, she has been concerned with the expression of self in words. But when words fail, her "self" begins to fall apart. Anna's disintegration is tied up with the whole question of the existence of individual consciousness: what makes up a "self," and what holds it together? The creation of Anna in *The Golden Notebook* is of a character accessible through words—her own words. She is never described by anyone else; no one peers into her consciousness and interprets it. Yet Anna's attempt at self-definition slowly collapses because it hinges on the power of words, and words cannot contain a reality too immense for them. At one point in her blue notebook she realizes:

> I am increasingly afflicted by vertigo where words mean nothing. Words mean nothing. They have become, *when I think*, not the form into which experience is shaped, but a series of meaningless sounds, like nursery talk, and away to one side of experience. Or like the sound track of a film that has slipped its connection with the film. *When I am thinking* I have only to write a phrase like "I walked down the street," or take a phrase from a newspaper "economic measures which lead to the full use of..." and immediately the words dissolve, and my mind starts spawning images which have nothing to do with the words, so that every word I see or hear seems like a small raft bobbing about on an enormous sea of images. So I can't write any longer. Or only when I write fast, without looking back at what I have written. For if I look back, then the words swim and have no sense and I am conscious only of me, Anna, as a pulse in a great darkness, and the words that I, Anna, write down are nothing, or like the secretions of a caterpillar that are forced out in ribbons to harden in the air.
>
> It occurs to me that what is happening is a breakdown of me, Anna, and this is how I am becoming aware of it. For words are form, and if I am at a pitch where shape, form, expression are

16. *The Summer before the Dark* contains Doris Lessing's most complex treatment of the whole subject of words: symbols, slogans, clichés, ritualistic utterances that shape and condition individual behavior.

nothing, then I am nothing, for it has become clear to me, reading the notebooks, that I remain Anna because of a certain kind of intelligence. This intelligence is dissolving and I am very frightened. [Pp. 407–8]

Anna is dissolving, and as she dissolves, the boundaries between what she has defined as her own consciousness and the consciousness of others become blurred. The sensitivity which has allowed her to receive so many impressions (note that the term "receive" implies that perception is passive) also allows her to receive emotions. Her self-identity has become so amorphous that what she receives *becomes* part of herself. As a consciousness not totally self-contained, it displays within it the disorder and confusion of the world outside. But outside and inside are losing their meaning. Thus during her intense affair with Saul Green, Anna begins to take on his mental illness. It takes great effort on her part even to recognize the merging of emotions: "I was clenched with anxiety, and saying over and over again: This isn't my anxiety state, it isn't mine—didn't help at all" (p. 486). Anna's absorption of Saul's sickness resembles, if in a more limited way, Martha's absorption of Lynda's insanity in *The Four-Gated City*. But Martha's evolution of consciousness goes much further. By now, the interpenetration of consciousnesses may be considered no longer a weakness but a precious ability which foresees the future course of human evolution.

The entire concept of ego undergoes a tremendous change by the time one gets to *The Four-Gated City*. Thus, if one considers *The Golden Notebook* as Doris Lessing's last attempt to define consciousness as self-contained, even that definition falters when Anna's attempt to fit the pieces of her life together fails because consciousness breaks out of its containers. The shared madness of Anna and Saul provides a new starting point.

Nonetheless, the very structure of *The Golden Notebook*, with its innumerable stories within stories, expresses what Doris Lessing meant by her comment that "the shape of this book should be enclosed and claustrophobic—so narcissistic that the subject matter must break through the form."[17] As Martha Quest discovered,

17. Schleuter, pp. 151–52.

nothing is as narcissistic as a pregnant woman, since she lives completely within herself. It is even as if the enclosed quality of *The Golden Notebook* might be said to resemble those symbols of pregnancy enumerated by Simone de Beauvoir when she spoke of children's love "of dolls that contain other similar dolls, of boxes containing other boxes, of pictures that contain replicas of decreasing size."[18] Moreover, there is an abundance of organic imagery in *The Golden Notebook,* and an emphasis on the sexual, reproductive capacities of its main character.

But the narcissistic, individualistic ego which accompanies a body that desires to take in, to hold on to, and to be made pregnant, is in *The Four-Gated City* replaced by a body that is a "machine" (p. 35) and a psyche which is "nothing but a soft dark receptive intelligence" (p. 36). The contained consciousness becomes consciousness as *receiver,* and Martha discovers "that somewhere in one's mind was a wavelength, a band where music jigged and niggled, with or without words; it was simply a question of tuning in and listening" (p. 37). "Tuning in and listening," then, defines the function of the individual mind.

But in order to "tune in," one must have the equipment with which to do so. Martha reflects that "living was simply a process of developing different 'ears,' senses, with which one 'heard,' experienced, what one couldn't before" (p. 225). Furthermore, the mind expansion revealed through the powers of ESP corresponds with a universal expansion. Martha knows that "she was not alone, others were feeling the same, since the growing point was never, could never be, just Martha's, could not be only the property or territory of one individual" (p. 486). No, what is going on is an evolutionary process (and here the old theme of determinism is used in a new context), and Doris Lessing quotes from *The Sufis* to explain how "*organs come into being as a result of a need for specific organs. . . . What ordinary people regard as sporadic and occasional bursts of telepathic and prophetic power are seen by the Sufi as nothing less than the first stirrings of these same organs*" (p. 426).

18. Simone de Beauvoir, *The Second Sex,* tr. and ed. H. H. Parshley (1949; reprinted, New York: Bantam Books, 1961), p. 265.

Human beings need these new organs to transcend time and space; thus within this context of mind expansion the subject of "words," so troubling to Anna Wulf when she became frustrated by her failure as a writer to explain her life, takes on a new interpretation. Anna had looked upon words as containers of experience, but for Martha in *The Four-Gated City*, words no longer enclose meaning but are used as *initiators* into the search for it. They have become catalysts, or powers which conduct meaning. They even retain some of their old use as magic: words which act like the mystic symbols in ancient and occult religions. Consequently, when Martha begins to "overhear" the thoughts of others, she discovers that words in themselves have no inherent meanings: "Was what she picked up words in its original form? Or did some mechanism exist which could pick up an idea, rather than words, from Paul's brain, Mark's, and translate it into words —like one of those simultaneous translators at a conference. Or like . . . a kind of computer that changed one language into another" (p. 353). The references to "simultaneous translators"[19] and "computers" serve to intensify the imagery of electronics even more obviously here than in their earlier connection with sexuality.

But if "developing different ears" implies a kind of passivity, paradoxically the process of doing so involves great effort: "this business of charting the new territory meant a continual painful effort of discovery, of trying to understand, to link, to make sense, and then falling back again, 'forgetting'; and then an effort forward again—a baby trying to walk" (p. 473). It is all in keeping with the struggle to connect individual and communal consciousness— a process of communication: "It is not a question of 'Lynda's mind' or 'Martha's mind'; it is the human mind, or part of it, and Lynda, Martha, can choose to plug it or not" (p. 473).

One might ask, then, what is it that one plugs into? The following passage may give at least a partial answer when it sets forth the unbelievable chaos and energy of what is approached when the mind is opened:

19. Kate Brown literally becomes a "simultaneous translator" at a conference in *Summer before the Dark*.

It was as if a million radio sets ran simultaneously, and her mind plugged itself in fast to one after another, so that words, phrases, songs, sounds, came into audition and then faded. The jumble and confusion were worse when she allowed the current that pumped through her to get out of control, to rise and jerk and flood; the sea of sound became more manageable as she held herself quiet and contained. Yet even so, it was all she could do to hold on . . . her own body bucking and rolling under her; and words, shrieks, gunfire, explosions, sentences, came in, faded, or stayed. When something stayed then it, they, might develop or grow loud and accumulate around it other words, sounds, phrases, of the same kind or texture, like a bit of metal attracting to it particles of substances of a certain nature, so that a word, "bread," proliferated into the phrase "bread of life," burst into a pure high song like a thrush, from the Ninth Symphony, then jangled into banality with "you can't have bread with one meat ball," gave snatches of recipes for loaves as they were once made on a hearth, leered, jeered, threatened, on a wavelength of mockery, until suddenly—while Martha understood (again) how the words, phrases, sounds, came in from that sound-length in an exact relation to some mood or impulse in herself. . . . [Pp. 473–74]

Martha's intuitive powers reach their climax with her achievement of extrasensory perception, but she had shown indications of an ability to perceive spontaneously and insightfully into the essence of a situation or character long before she embarked on that program of rigorous training: being alone, not eating, not sleeping, in order to make her mind completely open and sensitive to stimuli. Since adolescence she had been able to hold many perceptions in her mind at once, and to understand immediately the significance of a complex aggregation of details. It is the same ability Dorothy Richardson's Miriam Henderson attributed to the feminine consciousness; it is the same kind of understanding that marks the consciousness of all the female characters in this study. But Doris Lessing's use of this capability differs somewhat from the others. Fundamentally, the difference relates not to the powers themselves but to the interpretation of their meaning. This is a question of a difference in world views. Miriam Henderson achieved what she called "featureless freedom," a sense of oneness with a universe that ultimately seems to lack the concept of evil, predicated as it was upon the Quaker belief in the basic goodness of human beings. For Martha Quest, responding to the horrors of mid-twentieth-century history, such a view would be too simplistic. Doris Lessing does not allow her characters this kind of religious alternative; theirs is a world without God (and this gives it a much harsher quality of determinism than what marked Mary Olivier's), and life in itself has no spiritual meaning. Yet the same mental capabilities which allowed for religious experience in Miriam and Mary exist nonetheless.

Martha's adolescent moment of insight early in the *Children of Violence* series does share some of the features of Mary Olivier's penetration into reality (especially the clarity of vision, the sharply delineated objects), but the "secret happiness" which Mary radiated is different. The language is that of spiritual awakening: "it passed as lightly as the shadow of a wing" (*Martha Quest*, p. 50); "she knew that the experience associated with that emotion was not to be courted. One did not lie in wait for it; it was a visitor who came without warning" (p. 50). Martha recognizes the emotion as religious, yet she is no longer religious. The experience seems part of an innate capability, not related to belief. She stands looking across the dusty African landscape, quietly, expectant, the air blue and the grass rustling, and she observes two bucks in the sunlight. She questions the usual terms for her feelings—"ecstasy" and "illumination" both seem inadequate "because they suggest joy"—and she perceives it as "a pain, not a happiness" (p. 52).

> There was certainly a definite point at which the thing began. It was not; then it was suddenly inescapable, and nothing could have frightened it away. There was a slow integration, during which she, and the little animals, and the moving grasses, and the sun-warmed trees . . . and great dome of blue light overhead, and the stones of earth under her feet, became one, shuddering together in a dissolution of dancing atoms. She felt the rivers under the ground forcing themselves painfully along her veins, swelling them out in an unbearable pressure; her flesh was the earth, and suffered growth like a ferment; and her eyes stared, fixed like the

eye of the sun. Not for one second longer . . . could she have borne it; but then, with a sudden movement forwards and out, the whole process stopped; and *that* was "the moment" which it was impossible to remember afterwards. For during that space of time (which was timeless) she understood quite finally her smallness, the unimportance of humanity. . . . [Pp. 52–53]

Intuitive, visionary powers are part of the "feminine consciousness" as it has been defined by the women in these novels, but only Doris Lessing links these powers to a social vision. Martha's realization during "the moment" involves her insignificance in an "inhuman" universe. Her ego is inconsequential within "the chaos of matter." Her understanding involves an acceptance of the harshness of reality, which by contrast makes Miriam Henderson's vision of immensity seem cozy.

Moreover, it is not only the indifference of the universe to human desires that disturbs Martha, but that everywhere she looks she sees the indifference of one human being to another. There is a special warp to her consciousness; it has been affected by more than the philosophical theories about the absence of God and evolutionary determinism in the books she has read. The cataclysmic events of the twentieth century force her to see that the disorders in the political and social arenas are linked with universal forces which are revealed through the interactions of particles of matter, seasons, and movements of planets: massive powers that Martha intimated during her "moment." What is charging through them all charges through her own body: "Martha did not believe in violence. Martha was the essence of violence, she had been conceived, bred, fed and reared on violence" (*Landlocked*, p. 195).

The sexual dilemma which troubles Martha and Anna becomes part of this larger conflict as well. That "vision of some dark, impersonal destructive force that worked at the roots of life and that expressed itself in war and cruelty and violence" (*The Golden Notebook*, p. 164) is exemplified in the war between the sexes, which in Anna's own life comes to its climax in her violent struggles with Saul Green: "And I knew that the cruelty and the spite and the I, I, I, I, of Saul and of Anna were part of the logic of war . . ." (p. 503).

The forces of destruction are overwhelming, and they affect a feminine consciousness which is not only visionary and prophetic but idealistic as well. Martha's fantasies of a "four-gated city" represent the hope that there may be something different in the world than what is determined by the course of social history. Thus Anna tells her psychoanalyst that she feels something new in her life that does not correspond with the Jungian archetypes: "I believe I'm living the kind of life women never lived before." When the therapist insists that "the details change, but the form is the same," Anna says:

> . . . I don't want to be told when I suddenly have a vision (though God knows it's hard enough to come by) of a life that isn't full of hatred and fear and envy and competition every minute of the night and the day that this is simply the old dream of the golden age brought up to date. . . . No, because the dream of the golden age is a million times more powerful because it's possible, just as total destruction is possible. Probably *because* both are possible. . . . I want to be able to separate in myself what is old and cyclic, the recurring history, the myth, from what is new, what I feel or think that might be new. . . . [Pp. 403–4]

VI The deepest levels of Anna's consciousness are approached through dreams,[20] and it is in the final dreams described in her "golden" notebook that she begins to envision a merging of people, ideas, and emotions to take the place of the fragmentation implicit in the other notebooks. Not that the problem of internal chaos is resolved; but all the elements of confusion are, nevertheless, brought into relation with each other in a new way through the suggestion of cinematic form. After struggling to pull her many selves together, a new character enters Anna's dreams,

---

20. Doris Lessing's interest in dreams continues throughout her recent fiction: e.g., Kate Brown's recurrent and progressive dream about herself and the lost, helpless seal in *The Summer before the Dark*. Doris Lessing's comments to Jonah Raskin about her own use of dreams is especially illuminating. See Jonah Raskin, "Doris Lessing at Stony Brook: An Interview," *New American Review*, 8 (1970), 172–73.

a "projectionist" who takes control of her images and runs them before her eyes. Scene after scene from her life flashes by, image after image caught in close-up: "Then the film went very fast, it flicked fast, like a dream, on faces I've seen once in the street, and have forgotten, on the slow movement of an arm . . . all saying the same thing—the film was now beyond my experience, beyond Ella's, beyond the notebooks, because there was a fusion, and instead of seeing separate scenes, people, faces, movements, glances, they were all together . . ." (*The Golden Notebook*, p. 543).

Throughout the novel there are references to film, and these suggest an artistic evolution which puts Anna's attempts at ordering chaos through writing into a new perspective. The "fusion" which goes beyond her own experience is reminiscent of Eisenstein's comment: "It is only in cinema that are fused into a real unity all those separate elements of the spectacle once inseparable in the dawn of culture."[21] What is "fused" is "the full embrace of the whole inner world of man . . . a whole reproduction of the outer world."[22] Aside from its ability to incorporate everything, film is a powerful medium in that its images are *shared*, thus taking it beyond the individualism of the novel. Moreover, perhaps it, as a medium, has more potentiality for communicating what has been defined as the "feminine consciousness" because it may present the simultaneous experience of reality, the innumerable impressions within a moment of time, the inner and outer worlds so intertwined in consciousness, which all these writers have tried to express.

What her dreamed film achieves for Anna that her own interpretations through writing have not is the true perspective of her individual ego to the larger world. The "narcissism" of her own attempt to analyze herself and study herself within the enclosures of fictional forms thus is broken through. Anna then understands "courage" in a new light: "It's a small painful sort of courage which is at the root of every life, because injustice and cruelty is at the root of life. And the reason why I have only given my attention

21. Sergei Eisenstein, *Film Forum*, ed. and tr. Jay Leyda (New York: Meridian Books, 1957), p. 182.
22. *Ibid.*, p. 184.

to the heroic or the beautiful or the intelligent is because I won't accept the small endurance that is bigger than anything" (pp. 543–44).

The consciousness of the women in these novels is on the verge; elements of biological and cultural conditioning have gone into what has been considered a "feminine" consciousness, made up of passivity, submissiveness, resentment against men, and disassociation between body and mind. Kate Brown, looking beyond the years of motherhood, finally understands how she and other women have been programmed like "machines set for one function, to manage and arrange and adjust and foresee and order and bother and worry and organise. To fuss" (*The Summer before the Dark*, p. 105). But what lies ahead is some slight possibility of freedom, which in this context, at least, means *choosing* a new direction: a heightened notion of expanded consciousness which is not particularly "masculine" or "feminine" but human. Martha, when reaching new areas in herself, realizes "the sense of herself which stayed had no sex" (*The Four-Gated City*, p. 221).

Shifting her focus for a change to the consciousness of a male character in *Briefing* might in itself be a statement of Doris Lessing's desire to take her characters beyond conditioned roles. But even though the issue of sexuality seems to have been eliminated in *Briefing* (which moves its characters into worlds close to those of science fiction), it is still the puzzle of human consciousness that confronts us. Again we seem to plunge deep, deep within the layers of the mind. But we go even further here; we observe the consciousness of a man who has lost his "memory," who is supposed to be "mentally ill." The man himself, Charles Watkins, remains shadowy, incomplete, vague—impersonal. Yet this very impersonality helps one to discover that the entire concept of "personality" has changed. Tendencies, insights, perceptions that were revealed only in bits and pieces in the earlier novels are now carried to their firmest conclusion. For by now the feminine consciousness has disintegrated, and the idea of individual consciousness itself has been radically altered.

Doris Lessing attempts to express here the sense of a unity pervading the universe, moving with the forces of light and water and the planets and stars, to express that which is not yet completely understood, "the main feature of these human beings as at present constituted being their inability to feel, or understand themselves, in any other way except through their own drives or functions" (*Briefing*, p. 141). As in *The Four-Gated City* and *The Summer before the Dark*, Doris Lessing attempts to awaken humans who "have not yet evolved into an understanding of their individual selves as merely parts of a whole, first of all humanity, their own species, let alone achieving a conscious knowledge of humanity as part of Nature; plants, animals, birds, insects, reptiles, all these making a small chord in the Cosmic Harmony" (*Briefing*, p. 141).

Charles Watkins may be "insane" according to his doctors' definitions, but those definitions result from a scientific mentality which expresses its own limitations through its "inability to see things except as facets and one at a time" (*Briefing*, p. 142). Charles, on the other hand, sees now all at once, and not only are his concepts of time and space altered, but he begins to understand the interrelationships between all things: "I watched a pulsing swirl of all being, continually changing, moving, dancing, a controlled impelled dance, held within its limits by its nature" (p. 107). Once inside this other dimension, he understands how individual minds "lay side by side, fishes in a school, cells in honeycomb, flames in fire" (p. 106), and he perceives a "fusion with the people who were friends, companions, lovers and associates, a wholeness because I was stuck like a bit of coloured glass in a mosaic" (p. 106).

Consequently, that individual consciousness which Anna Wulf saw as "a pulse in a great darkness" loses its connotations of alienation. Although Charles's own mind might be felt as "a pulse of individuality" (*Briefing*, p. 112), yet "pulses of mind lay beating and absorbing beside my own little pulse, and together we were a whole" (p. 112). Moreover, in itself "humanity was a pulse in the life of the Sun" (p. 116), thus extending again the dimensions of the metaphor and using it to serve as the connection between the single consciousness and the evolving consciousness of the world.

Conclusion

MARTHA QUEST is dead by the end of Doris Lessing's *The Four-Gated City*. Her *Bildungsroman* has come to its end and with it, perhaps, the whole notion of "feminine consciousness" as it has developed over the more than fifty years since an adolescent Miriam Henderson set out on her journey to Hanover. Miriam, revealing herself as optimistic, open, and enthusiastic about the possibilities life offers a young woman seeking independence, would have been incapable of imagining the fate of her later counterpart. Martha also makes a journey, but hers takes her first to a dying England and last to a remote island where survivors of an atomic holocaust struggle to maintain life. Yet the two women began their search for reality in ways not at all dissimilar: reading iconoclastic authors, questioning the beliefs and values of their societies, living alone in the city, experimenting with sexual relationships. But their conclusions reflect the vast differences in their worlds. Miriam's discovery involves an assertion of the superiority of a feminine consciousness which allows her to accept and enhance essentially mystical and individualistic notions about the self. But Martha reaches the limits of self-concern; she discovers a social world, a political world, and a communal consciousness. Her individualism is tempered by world-wide historical changes, the coming end of the known civilization.

Long before her death she is aware of her insignificance, and the very struggle for some kind of identity that is specifically female is left far behind.

Miriam and Martha represent the extremes of this study, the opposite ends in time and concept. But even those characters who fall between them—Mary Olivier, Clarissa Dalloway, Olivia Curtis—characters more vulnerable and less assertive, serve to demonstrate women's growing conflict, the psychic tension which results from a split between the ideal of sexual equality and the reality of sexual subordination.

Throughout my reading of these novels I have been struck by the ingenuity with which these women have been able to define themselves as "feminine" according to concepts of femininity set down by men, at the same time that they rebel against the implications of such conceptions. Martha Quest's death, for all I know, may mark the end of this kind of self-defining. Although it would be difficult to predict the future course of any idea, especially as it becomes transformed in fiction, nevertheless, it does seem to me that if the nonfiction writing of the new feminists of the 1970s is any indication, women's new self-definitions will avoid any limitations of possibilities. The new feminists, especially the more radical among them, hope for a change in men that will correspond with their own de-emphasis of given characteristics. They would like to do away with the old notions entirely, so that even the traditionally positive values—intuition, sensitivity, tenderness—will be attributed not only to women but to men as well. What they speak about comes close to Dinah's comment about a new gender emerging, the breaking down of divisions between men and women.

But this study ends before the change is completed. The women in these novels are rebels in some cases, acquiescent wives in others, but they all recognize the difficulties of their roles. Afraid to be considered "masculine" in a society which labels intellect as a trait belonging to men, supported by a psychology which considers "anatomy as destiny," these very intelligent women—and intelligence and sensitivity are the characteristics *all* of them share—have developed notions of "feminine consciousness" which allow them to order their intellects into shapes which will be recognized as "feminine." It calls for some trickery, some self-deception, but they manage to do it.

Their definitions of "feminine consciousness" are part of, and in some cases synonymous with, their search for reality. They aim for a true sense of self-autonomy and need to fight against being considered objects and mere passive beings. But since so many of society's values have been incorporated within their own consciousnesses, their struggle is never completely successful. Conventional standards of feminine behavior such as self-sacrifice, modesty, maternality, and submission go right along with those passive tendencies which society has defined as the real feminine virtues. So in their relations with men—relations that appear to get increasingly strained the further one goes in the period—these women often submit, give in, and lose out. For it does become quite obvious when looking at the men in these novels (and a most important part of the feminine consciousness is the awareness of men as seen through women's eyes) that the conventional standards for "masculinity" are as much at odds with reality as women's standards for themselves.

The inner struggle regarding men takes various forms in these novels, sometimes denying passivity, other times elevating it. A woman might assume a male role for a short time, falling in love with another woman (as do Miriam, Clarissa, and Judith), or she might act with hostility toward men and ceaselessly argue with them, or she might act with surface submissiveness but reveal a consciousness torn with anger and resentment. On the other hand, the attempt to elevate passive qualities by identifying with processes of nature, by self-sacrifice, is equally apparent. But what seems to me most significant, in that it reveals how truly difficult is the struggle, is the ironic similarity among these women in ending their battle. One after the other ultimately rejects men. Proceeding toward asexual and mystical solutions, Miriam finds "featureless freedom," Mary a "secret happiness" in giving up her own desires to the will of God, Clarissa a separate bedroom, and Martha the absorption in extrasensory perception.

To defend their position—and it must be remembered that the

feminine consciousness is itself a defensive construction—these women insist that the thought processes of women are different from those of men. Miriam, recognizing women's ability to perceive the diversity of reality simultaneously (an apprehension not time-centered), believes men are so caught up in the processes of "becoming" that they are only able to keep one thing in their minds at a time, thus explaining their predilection for categorizing "life" and ordering it into hierarchies. Clarissa also opposes the rationality of men to her own delicate perceptions, to her sense of the diffuseness of consciousness and the great mystery of existence. Olivia notices the superficiality of men's conceptualizations, and Martha men's conventionality. It all adds up to a respect for the intuitive, the spontaneous, the diverse, the complexly simple. And it indicates a rather profound radicalism at the heart of their definitions, since through the assertion of the value of the inner being opposed to the outer, these women reject authority. Even Clarissa Dalloway, snobbish though she may be in some ways, nonetheless deflates the pomposity of authoritative men.

Sometimes the strain of battle becomes overwhelming, however, and then one notices the retreat into a rather stereotyped fantasy of a golden past, a time when women were supposed to have had a real, necessary role. To complement that vision is one of an old-fashioned, strong, "masculine" man, whose aggressiveness supports the inner placidity of "his" woman. Thus Miriam has moments when she dreams of life as the mysterious center of a home with Dr. Densley, or living close to nature on a farm with Richard Roscorla. Olivia has a vision of herself in a cottage, caring for her "love child." Even Martha Quest, the most contemporary, the "free-est" sexually and socially, imagines as her alter ego a black farm woman, bearing a child a year, as the representative of a culture still bound up in the cycles of nature. And the very character of Mrs. Ramsay epitomizes in their purest form the traditional "feminine" values. Her whole being symbolizes the woman whose life is centered in her family.

But such retreats into the past are transient ones, coming and going with the strains of modern life. Their part in the feminine consciousness is a remnant—disturbing and intriguing, reminding of lost possibilities—not feasible any longer because the alert, self-centered consciousnesses of these women are not in tune with a traditional way of living. They are searching for "reality," and their reality must include a recognition of their own autonomy.

Index